You Better T-H-I-N-K

Before You Speak!

You Better T-H-I-N-K
Before You Speak!

PAMELA D. FOSTER

LueMil Publishing

Copyright © 2025 Pamela D. Foster;
YOU BETTER THINK BEFORE YOU SPEAK
Second Edition: 2025

ISBN: 978-0-9987686-4-9
ISBN: 978-0-9987686-5-6 (ePub)
LCCN: 2024921906

Published by LueMil Publishing
216 W Fort Toulouse Road #503
Wetumpka, AL 36093

Visit the author's website at
http://www.pameladfoster.com
Email: pamdfos@gmail.com
Twitter: @PamelaDFos

This book or parts thereof may not be reproduced in any form, stored in a retrieval system or transmitted in any form by any means—electronic, mechanical, photocopy, recording or otherwise without prior written permission or the publisher, except as provided by United States of America copyright law.

Unless otherwise noted, verses are cited from THE HOLY BIBLE, NEW INTERNATIONAL VERSION®, NIV® Copyright © 1973, 1978, 1984, 2011 by Biblica, Inc.® Used by permission. All rights reserved worldwide.

Scripture quotations marked KJV are from the King James Version of the Bible.

"Scripture quotations taken from the Amplified® Bible (AMP), Copyright © 2015 by The Lockman Foundation

Used by permission. www.Lockman.org"

Scripture quotations marked (NLT) are taken from the Holy Bible, New Living Translation, copyright © 1996, 2004, 2007 by Tyndale House Foundation. Used by permission of Tyndale House Publishers, Inc., Carol Stream, Illinois 60188. All rights reserved.

Scripture quotations marked HCSB are taken from the Holman Christian Standard Bible®, Copyright © 1999, 2000, 2002, 2003, 2009 by Holman Bible Publishers. Used by permission. Holman Christian Standard Bible®, Holman CSB®, and HCSB® are federally registered trademarks of Holman Bible Publishers.

Scripture quotations marked (ABPE) are taken from the ARAMAIC BIBLE IN PLAIN ENGLISH, 2010 Copyright©, Rev. David Bauscher, Lulu Enterprises Incorporated, 2010

The Holy Bible: International Standard Version. Release 2.0, Build 2015.02.09. Copyright © 1995-2014 by ISV Foundation. ALL RIGHTS RESERVED INTERNATIONALLY. Used by permission of Davidson Press, LLC.

Printed in the United States of America

Morris and Sarah:

Momma and Daddy, though you are no longer here on earth, your presence is still felt every day. Thank you for life, love, and believing in me...

Still missing you

Contents

PREFACE ix
INTRODUCTION xv

Part 1 Do You THINK? 1
T – true 3
H – helpful 23
I – inspiring 43
N – necessary 55
K – kind 69
S – season 89

Part 2 You Should... 107
Why? 109

Part 3 Barriers... 127
Barriers 129

CONCLUSION 141
REFERENCES 145
ABOUT THE AUTHOR 147

PREFACE

Years have passed between this second edition, "You Better Think Before You Speak," and the first. Since then, friends, family, and readers have wondered when the next book will come out. Well *life started lifing* and here we are. After public engagement requests from local organizations, I thought it was best to tweak some ideas and elaborate on principles before presenting this book again.

Allow me to give you some history. Years ago, I was introduced to the THINK acronym while preparing to teach a Christian youth education class. While teaching this communication principle, I knew it would be valuable and applicable to my life and the teenagers. It was simple yet direct enough for them to comprehend and connect, so I knew I would revisit it. Fast-forward a couple of years, and I began to discuss it on Periscope.

This book is based on the Periscope series I presented, *"You Better Think Before You Speak."* As I shared these principles combined with biblical scriptures, there was such a tremendous response that I further developed and enhanced the teaching. I realized this topic of interest needed to be expounded on and put in an actual book for my Periscope viewers and non-social media users.

IS THIS BOOK FOR YOU?

Okay, you know how this book came about, but you might still wonder if this book is for you. Well, who is this book for? If you like reading simple, compact, and straight-to-the-point books, it's for you. Have you ever found yourself in a pickle/jam/situation because of the words you spoke? If the answer is yes, this book is for you. Any person willing to examine/re-examine their thought life and develop it should read this book.

You don't have to be an individual of faith to enjoy and glean a nugget of wisdom—just someone willing to learn. The beautiful thing about life is that everyone has something to offer, and you can absorb knowledge from many sources. Be a sponge and learn what you can. Whether you are a high school student, judge, entertainer, stay-at-home parent, or chef, you can and will benefit from a mindset overhaul. I needed one, and that's another reason I penned this book.

"You Better Think Before You Speak" was also birthed out of a desire to strengthen, appreciate, and be productive in my purpose and fulfill destiny. Purpose is the reason God has me on earth, and destiny is the culmination of that journey. Like countless others before me, I realize that divine success

is about more than getting there (the place of purpose and destiny).

I imagine it's like marriage. I guess because I've never been married, and be it far from me to lecture those of you who have leaped into wedded bliss or torture, depending on whom you chose as a mate. **<u>ANYONE</u>** can get married!

Maturity is understanding you don't know it all...there's always someone with greater insight.

Did you see the emphasis on "anyone"? All you need is a person willing to say yes and agree to stay together (or at least promise), money to pay for the licenses, an appointment at the courthouse, a state official to authenticate it, and voila, you are married.

However, it takes <u>work</u> to stay married or be in any relationship, and each party must commit to it. Judging by the high divorce rate not just in the United States but in the Western hemisphere, one party isn't/wasn't interested in the "work" piece of the deal. If one side doesn't want to make it work, it won't!

Just as it takes a concerted effort to be married, it also takes hard work to be a better person (in all facets, including communication) and advance in life. You can develop and reach the pinnacle by staying the course, but it's really about the ability to maintain when you have arrived. Many people get to the top but don't have the tools or capacity to stay.

Look at the voracious news cycle, and you'll see some of your favorite celebrities hitting the pinnacle of success but "fall from fame" shortly after. They were skilled at their craft but didn't know how to harness those skills, gifts, talents, and abilities. You must possess more than talent. The staying power comes by having the following:

- **Tenacity** — Tenacity is weathering and learning from storms that *will* come into your life. Storms are not partial or optional. Just as they naturally build and erupt across a region or country, they will pass over your life. They come and go and turn things upside down, blow away, and uproot. We are to allow that storm to process and refine us. The refining happens when you persevere, not quit before you've comprehended the life lesson being taught and are ready to move on to the next step of your purpose.

- **Character** — Character is choosing to stay above board, not cheating, lying, backstabbing, participating in immoral or illegal activities, or acting unseemly. As the spotlight is shone on you, do you change and do the opposite like that is your usual mode of operation? That is not character. Who are you when no one is watching? Not when a crowd is present to give you a high five for doing the right thing. The real test is when no one can hear or see you do things that, if found out, would make you hang your head in shame and blush furiously. Character doesn't care who is around; it continually seeks integrity and justice.

- **Wisdom** — It's the key to knowing what to do with what you have and acquiring more of what you need. Consider a famous and financially stable celebrity who may have the gift and ability but lacks wisdom. Raw talent opens doors, but understanding helps to maintain and solidify them. Wisdom guides us to use our gifts in the right season and place. It's futile to be out of season and unprepared, just as reaching purpose without understanding can be dangerous. It's like depleting resources meant for another season and mishandling precious gifts. Using talents and abilities judiciously ensures readiness, proper impact, and influence in your realm.

- **Gracious speech** — Great discourse is borne of experience, practice, and maturity. Boy, do I remember the days my dialogue wasn't necessarily ungracious, but it was lacking. I've always been mindful of other's feelings and, consequently, what I've said, but there's something about the passage of time, like a fine wine, that becomes better with age. Time produces quality, understanding, compassion, and wisdom. These attributes materialize through living life and maturing. Wise speakers are mature enough to forego what their emotions desire and see the big picture of what lies ahead. You're not genuinely gracious in your speech until you've lived a little and experienced the good and bad life offers. We all know time and experience are the best teachers. You can't learn lessons from a scripted textbook; only life can give them.

Tenacity, character, wisdom, and grace are interdependent and vital to progress. Gracious speaking is the consummation and outward manifestation of the other three. I will focus on—using the T-H-I-N-K principle to help you become a more courteous and gracious speaker. I'm talking about you, reader, a person of excellence whose communication will further enhance and develop your personal and business life. I hope the following pages encourage you as much as they encouraged me and those who patiently listened daily on Periscope (a now-defunct social media platform). So, settle down, grab a cup of your favorite tea or a coffee, and let's go on a journey together.

INTRODUCTION

Since the days of old, humans have been practicing and mindful of presenting their finest communications. Nobility, namely kings, had advisers who rendered services, including political and social advice, and could sometimes be confidantes. This individual ensured that the king's best face and voice were shown to the public.

The equivalent today would be a public relations (PR) firm. Almost every sizeable organization has an in-house or on-call PR team, whether in the entertainment industry, sports, politics, military, governmental sector, or other fields. Those old enough will remember some of the biggest scandals within the past 20 to 30 years originating in the United States but broadcast worldwide: Bill Clinton and Monica Lewinsky, O.J. Simpson and Nicole Brown, Michael Jackson, and the Neverland accusers.

The above-mentioned high-profile individuals retained a team of professionals who worked to sway public opinion in their favor. Image consultants advised them on what to wear and acceptable grooming tips commensurate with their predicament and gave them carefully worded, rehearsed speeches to spout on television. Much of what we saw then and today is a finely crafted image. Those with means can afford to pay to have others speak for and about them.

As for us regular folks, you and I don't have the luxury of doling out thousands and even millions (depending on the severity of the problem and how deep your pockets are) to put us back in the right standing if we misspeak or mess up. Or pay for a medical bill if our words land us in urgent care or a hospital. Let's hope it doesn't get that far ☺. As with any growth experience, we must change our mindset.

Thinking New

There is not one person, living or dead, that hasn't contracted and suffered from the deadly "foot in mouth disease" at least once, twice, or a hundred times in their life. I know this ailment has plagued me in the past, and I still trip up now and then…and I'm sure (no, make that "know") you've been afflicted as well. Foot-in-mouth disease is the condition where you say something, and then as those words pass your lips, you realize it was better left unsaid. Not that it was intentional or meant to injure, but it was still one of those rolling-off-the-tongue moments that made you look like a simpleton.

You wanted (and I) to take the words back in the worst or best way in this case. However, the damage had been done, and we left the conversation with our proverbial tails tucked between our legs due to our inability to thoughtfully consider and manage our words through the T-H-I-N-K filter. We must decide if our conversation is True, Helpful, Inspiring, Necessary, and Kind before we allow it to pass our lips into the atmosphere.

Proverbs 21:23 New Living Translation (NLT) tells us, *"Watch your tongue and keep your mouth shut, and you will stay out of trouble."* We stay out of trouble when considering how our words will impact and influence the person(s) receiving them. Damage control is a task no one wants to perform. It's better to measure your words in advance so you don't have to pay a high price later. Oh, how I wished I had heeded this sound proverb in times past, but you know human tendency. We all have 20/20 after the fact.

Imperfect human nature causes us to say the things we shouldn't and do things we don't want to. Paul, previously a staunch persecutor of Christians, said it best in Romans 7:15 (NIV), *"I do not understand what I do. For what I want to do, I do not do, but what I hate I do."* Paul is not excusing bad behavior but merely telling us it's delicate human nature that causes us to do foolish things or express those words we don't want to. Still, we do it anyway and immediately regret it.

You know, like telling loved ones a *piece* of your mind when you don't have any *peace* yourself and should keep the little left you have. The spirit man knows and wants to do what is right, but the flesh man is always tempted to obey base desires.

Base desires make us do and say things without thinking, which is the problem. We need to think before we speak! The

T-H-I-N-K acronym is a part of our next level of living. Next-level living is walking in a spirit of excellence. The spirit of excellence means every area of our life is governed by integrity and maturation. We intentionally and strategically live life for maximum impact.

Strategy means there is a plan of action to execute. There is a plan; we're not living haphazardly. You know the adage: *If you don't have a plan, you're planning to fail.* Failure is not an option for you or me. Nothing ought to be left to chance—including our speech.

The higher we advance, the more polished we should be, and there is no more significant indicator of this than the words and daily conversation we engage in. I sincerely wish those of you unfamiliar with the T-H-I-N-K concept will learn a new way of conversing, and those who already know it will leave with a jewel or two to apply in their daily lives. Why?

Life already presents its challenges, so there's no need to complicate it further with ill-spoken words and actions that do not serve their intended purpose. Thinking before speaking gives you and me a chance to consider the positive and negative effects of our words before, not after, the damage has been done.

Evaluate your thinking habits and be ready to change those that no longer benefit and enrich your character or life. Remember, next-level living is living in excellence. I'd also like to add "awareness." Be aware that some restructuring and shifting needs to take place for promotion. Keep an open mind and identify the areas of strength and weakness so you can move purposefully and fulfill your destiny. I can do it, and so can you.

READY... SET... THINK!

PART 1
Do You THINK?

T – true

"The LORD detests lying lips, but delights in people who are trustworthy."
Proverbs 12:22 (NIV)

Our everyday conversations allow others a first-hand look into who we truly are. The authenticity or integrity of that communication gives them an idea of whether we are reliable or someone to beware of. We must first be honest with ourselves before we can be honest with the world. What do I mean when I say be honest with yourself? Truth CAN, and often is, highly subjective, depending on a person's upbringing, ethics, and understanding of reality.

Hypothetically speaking, if you grow up in a household where truth changes daily or when convenient, you might lean towards creating your reality as you see fit. Anything that doesn't align with your idea of truth is discarded and replaced with something more palatable. You might have developed a sense of entitlement due to factors like financial status, skin color, gender, or intelligence scores.

Whoever didn't share those attributes and wasn't "on your level" might've been belittled or shunned. You would've excused your way of bias and thinking by rationalizing that *everyone else felt the same* and, therefore, it is true. Your version of the truth became fluid, shaped by your environment and experiences.

REALITY USED TO BE A FRIEND!

What is truth? Being in accordance with the actual state of affairs and conformable to an essential reality (Merriam Webster, 2024). I'm sure we all know at least one person who refuses to accept reality. I am a retired United States Air Force veteran and spent much of my career stationed overseas. On one of those assignments, I had the (dis)pleasure of working with a guy who had some serious issues with reality. He entertained the squadron with thinly veiled tall tales—or rather, outright lies on a near-daily basis. It depended on when he wasn't wasting the squadron's monthly gas allowance, running around the base feigning importance.

One delightful and bizarre tall tale was about him being the only soldier in his unit to contract a deadly blood-borne disease during wartime in Iraq. This alleged disease supposedly made him deathly ill and caused him to lose a significant amount of weight. Not only did he lose weight, but he also contracted gastrointestinal issues as well? Wouldn't you know it, these horrible gastro maladies included uncontrollable bowel movements and passing blood. As if that story wasn't weird enough, he then told the crowd of amused unbelieving people gathered around his desk that no one in his squadron or medical facility (at that previous location) believed he had a disease. Imagine that! Of course, since no one in that squadron would buy his Bunyanesque tale, he sought to prove everyone wrong.

You will not be considered credible if your words are never grounded in truth!

The story continues with him wanting to prove to his office that he wasn't crying wolf. He allegedly saved a large sample of human waste mixed with blood and drove it to the base hospital. After getting there, he threw it (yes, you read right— "it," of course, being the blood and feces) on the military hospital floor in front of the technician and asked, "Do you believe me now?" I know it was and is an outrageous story, and the sad part is that he stuck with it despite being challenged.

There is no way in the world he would've gotten away with that behavior and not be given a fancy new white suit, also known as a strait jacket, or be sedated somewhere in a padded room, or possibly be given discharge papers for mental instability and being an endangerment to his fellow service members. We endured so many wild stories that year. How about one more bizarre story just for chuckles and grins?

Truth exposes those who don't follow her instructions.

He also told co-workers and strangers alike that 12 men had beaten him up while he was home on leave (civilian equivalence of a vacation or holiday) at a club because they found out he was in the army, and they broke his neck in a fight. We already knew he was lying, and later, we surmised that the brand-new white neck brace he was sporting had been purchased at a local medical supply store in his hometown.

The brace was to serve three purposes, none of which he accomplished: garner sympathy, receive a medical profile to exempt him from physical training, and validate his deceptive nature. I could easily write chapters detailing the daily falsehoods this man told. Suffice it to say he was not grounded in truth and was treated as one to avoid and take lightly.

Let's look at another person. I knew a woman who denied being pregnant up until the seventh month of her pregnancy.

Sounds weird, right? When her stomach started protruding in her first trimester, she told everyone she was gaining weight. By the fourth month, she started saying she had some gastrointestinal issues.

Medical issues, probably because they are challenging to prove, seem to be a running theme and a constant go-to excuse for those unwilling to handle the truth and deal in the here and now. The last months couldn't be denied as her belly swelled up like a beach ball. She came clean and said she didn't realize she was pregnant.

I'm not saying it's impossible to be unaware of a baby growing inside you, as documented by the once popular and intriguing The Learning Channel (TLC) television show "*I Didn't Know I Was Pregnant.*" There have been genuine cases of women, particularly younger ones, who were completely oblivious that a child was forming in them.

They missed the signs because they still had a menstrual cycle or were told they could never have children. However, this woman reasoned she could deny her pregnancy away, out of existence, almost as if the constant denial would result in the embryo magically expelling itself from the body.

There comes a time when we must face facts and realism. Like many others, these two individuals felt that living in an alternate reality, not the actual one, makes it so. No, it doesn't; it further hampers you from dealing with present issues and possibly getting professional help.

💡 **NOTE:** If you need help, seek it! There is no shame in wanting to be whole in every area of your life, whether mental, physical, or financial. The shame lies in knowing you need to reach out but not doing so out of selfishness, apathy, or embarrassment. You have a right to live a whole life free of guilt, fear, and denial.

DENIAL, NOT THE NILE

For some people, denial means it's not true; it's not real. It's almost as if you deny it long enough, then you won't be held responsible or accountable. The pregnant woman must have believed that by repeating 'I'm not pregnant,' she could avoid future responsibility. The tall-tale co-worker aptly nicknamed "the patron saint of liars" might have surmised that it would eventually become a fact if he had lied enough. He wasn't one to bother with those pesky little details called truth. I suppose it's because 'everyone does it,' right?

High-profile cases of politicians, clergy, and entertainers trapped in denial and rebounding after creative public relations managers finesse the public only encourage the masses and fuel the flames of denial. The average person sees 'big-name people,' who are supposed to be respectable, getting away with it and thinks it's okay for them, too. When these prominent individuals get caught, they deny it.

There must be some unwritten code that, if caught, deny until proof surfaces and, when the evidence does come to light, declare, "It wasn't me." Even with a smoking gun in the palm of their hand, the "deniers" still deny. Like the innocent until proven guilty legal principle, these people act as if they are telling *the truth* unless you can prove they are not. "The phrase 'Deny, deny…you've still been caught in a lie!' comes to mind. Don't get it twisted. Truth is like a bulwark; no amount of denial can move it.

Ignoring the truth won't make the issue disappear in a puff of smoke. We are not Dorothy from The Wizard of Oz, and no amount of clicking together ruby red heels or dress shoes will change our situation—only TAKING strategic individual measures and ENACTING them will. Remember, it wasn't until Dorothy took decisive action in her dream that she could wake up and deal with her life in Kansas.

Closing your eyes and repeating there's no place like home only prolongs the process and keeps you in a place of stagnation. Inactivity leads to death. Have you ever walked by a stagnant pond or another body of water? You immediately know it's stagnant because of the smell. We want a living truth, not a dead one, based on our perception and approval. Fortunately, or unfortunately, depending on **your** stance, life doesn't work per our acceptance of events. I'm glad it doesn't, considering many would refuse to address uncomfortable problems because they don't *see* one.

I'm encouraging you to be upfront and stop shoving problems under the rug. Whether they are relational, business, health, or financial—deal with them. Digging your head in the proverbial sand doesn't bring you closer to a solution. You must be present in this world, face your problem(s) head-on, and resolve the unpleasant difficulties you are experiencing. Handle your problems, or your problems will handle you!

Ignoring the truth won't make your problems disappear. Face them or they will face you!

After we have addressed our predicaments (not ignored them), we become rooted in truthfulness and can start engaging the world. Telling the truth will become second nature because we live in truth. But what is truth? One definition is sincerity in action, character, and utterance.[1] That's the Webster's dictionary version. Since I like to simplify things, let me give you the plain English version per Pamela: truth means there is credible evidence backing up a declaration or statement. If it's fake or false, it's not true. It's either all true or all false.

A HALF-TRUTH IS A TOTAL LIE

I'm a big fan of classic 60s, 70s, and 80s television shows. The actors and actresses were (mostly) turning out stellar performances because they could really act—none of this tasteless, outlandish reality television rubbish we see today. My favorite scenes were always after a whodunit, where a well-dressed witness was sworn in, and the court officer asked, "Do you solemnly swear or affirm that you will tell the truth, the whole, and nothing but the truth, so help you, God?" It was dramatic and severe. That's a question we should ask ourselves before we speak.

Are we ensuring what comes out of our mouths is true, or do we play fast and loose, embellishing here and there to get things done or iron out a problem? Our friendly supply sergeant embodied this. He could tell a lie quicker than he could part his lips and wasn't afraid to add or subtract details to fit the narrative. You know how *we* do: act dishonest and say it was no biggie. The driver's license station clerk asks for your height/weight, and your response has you 20 pounds lighter and an inch taller. No harm, no foul, right? It's only a little white lie.

Of course, there's no such thing as a white lie. A lie is a lie. I wonder who came up with that phrase? Why not say a small lie which is still a lie? You can tell a significant or trivial one, which still doesn't change the fact that one was told. A "white lie" has been cloaked as an "itsy little bit" of a lie told with honest intention but a lie nonetheless. You may have the best intentions of not telling someone the truth, but you do more harm than good. That person might have learned a valuable lesson or gained vital experience. Instead, they remain in untruth. Let's look at these two scenarios and see if you'd tell the truth:

Scenario 1
Your close buddy wants to purchase a sporty, fast two-seater convertible—his lifelong dream car. He tells you how much it costs, and your eyes bulge out, wondering if he's lost his mind. You know, to afford it, he'll have to eat like a toddler for the next three years, stop paying the electric bill, and skip child support payments.

When he asks you if it's too expensive, do you tell him he can swing it because you feel sorry he's had a rough year—nasty divorce and impending hair loss, or do you tell him to get his head out of the clouds and take care of responsibilities?

Try this: "Dude, you have been through so much lately and deserve to treat yourself. But I don't want to see you under any more unnecessary stress. I've hated seeing you, my best friend, under that type of pressure. Why don't you hold off until you can pay for it in cash or make a sizeable downpayment? That way, you can enjoy that beauty without worry."

If he still acts a fool and purchases it anyway, you will have a clear conscience that you gave him wise counsel, and he disregarded it. So when he comes back, balder and crying that he can't make the payments, tell him you'll trail him as he drives that expensive liability back to the car lot and drops the keys off.

Scenario 2
A close female friend asks how she looks in a particular outfit, and you tell her it looks great. Your real thought is that her

appearance resembles a stuffed sausage. You said she looked awesome because you didn't want to hurt any already sensitive feelings. In hindsight, you might have been better off encouraging your best friend to change into something that suits her current size instead of the one she thinks she can fit into from high school.

You know beyond a shadow of a doubt she could only fit into those clothing if she died and maggots stripped her bones clean. Maybe I went a little too far, but you get the picture. There's no way those jeans are passing those thighs or gut. A friendly public service announcement: Friends don't let friends come out in public looking crazy. The next time you face this situation, don't allow your loved one to exit their home.

As a woman of age, I understand the importance of appropriately fitting clothing. You still want to dress modern, but not at the expense of a body that doesn't match the cut of said fashions.

Since dying and coming back to life to fit into an article of clothing is not feasible, you must work around their emotions and perceptions and present realism while being honest. That's a tall order, right?

Situational honesty doesn't work. It's best to keep quiet if you fear the consequences.

Try this: "Girl, that's a nice outfit, but I like this one on you. It has you snatched (translation: your body looks amazing, and it flatters your curves). Now, that's the one that makes a statement".

Or this one: "You've always had great taste in clothing and worn aesthetically pleasing outfits, but I like this pair of jeans because the cut flatters your curves (ladies) or physique (gentlemen). I think these jeans are the best fit." The statement was honest. You were candid without degrading their style; you were mindful of their feelings and are saving them from embarrassment. We're tempted to be untruthful to soften the blow, but who does that help? If you're not honest with your friend, someone else will be, and chances are they'll be brutal. Are you feeling more inclined to be honest now?

What's the moral, you ask? Telling the truth (with love) is always better than serving up a half-truth or sugar-coated lie. Let's not forget—a half-truth is still a lie. Mark Twain, the world-renowned and highly comical American writer, said a half-truth is the most cowardly of lies. It's cowardly to tell a half-truth because we refuse to address a situation or event, cover it up, and substitute it with a falsehood.

A coward can't be counted on to stand for justice when she calls.

Instead of facing the problem, we choose to sidestep it with the most amazing evasive tactics. That is not integral and corrupts our conversation and personal growth journey. Sometimes, it's okay to say nothing or, "I'm not sure about that; maybe ask someone with more expertise."

This refusal to own and take responsibility for our lives makes us cowards. Ouch! I've been one, and so have you. If you are living and breathing, you've displayed gutless actions at some point. I know that is harsh, but until we are ready to be truthful about where we are, we won't change. Some scenes are playing in my memory bank right now, and they're not ones of courage. You have some unsavory memories, too. No worries, friend, we've all fallen short, but we won't live in condemnation. Here's what we will do: forgive ourselves, turn away from the practice, and move on. See how simple that was?

Let's revisit that cowardice piece. What exactly do I mean when I say coward? A coward can't be counted on to stand for justice when she calls. Look back in history at social injustice through the marginalization of a group or nation, and you will find individuals, organizations, and institutions sitting/standing by without a care in the world. Meanwhile, discriminatory practices continued as usual in business, finance, education, and social settings. It wasn't until after brave souls stood up, protested, were jailed, and even died that legislation was enacted and attitudes shifted.

Whether it's a cowardly action or statement, the truth will come to either crown you with glory or bring shame to those who refuse to partake. Will you be shamed or crowned? You don't get a partial crown for telling a partial truth. It's all or nothing.

THE TRUTH IS THE TRUTH?

Part-time honesty or situational truth doesn't work, and it puts you on the path to unreliability, just like the supply sergeant I mentioned earlier. He was good for a laugh and distraction, but that was it. No one trusted him to perform tasks that involved credibility or judgment. He wasn't trusted—just tolerated because he could be used to make things happen (sometimes not legal or moral, if you catch my drift).

> Truth is like money in the bank. Either you have it or you don't.

I don't know if he intended to be known as the squadron liar because not too many people intentionally set out to ruin their reputation by being unreliable and truth-delinquent. Somewhere along the way, truth for him/others becomes fluid and interchangeable if the benefits outweigh the risks. Bending the truth and telling outright lies, no matter who gets hurt, is secondary to attaining money, fame, and power.

The question is, are those aspirations more important than honesty and integrity? For some, the answer is yes because chasing them (unbalanced ambitions) is addictive and probably just as deadly as crack cocaine. The more you consume an addictive substance, the more you crave it. Likewise, when chasing fame and money, you'll never be satisfied. It's a canyon that can't be filled. Find the fulfillment within you first, and it will translate to the external!

 ## WHAT'S THE LESSON?

What nuggets can we take away from this chapter? Truth is foundational to all things in life, especially speaking. We should first consider whether we are about to impart knowledge or foolishness. Hopefully, now you've decided that truth is where it's at. Are you ready to speak that truth—in love? Don't forget that part. Proverbs 27:6 (NLT) says, *"Wounds from a sincere friend are better than many kisses from an enemy."* Loose translation: Truth spoken in love from a friend, acquaintance, or stranger, even if unpleasant, is better than hearing lies from someone who doesn't have your best interest.

"We're adults, right? Picture this: You begin to fall asleep at the wheel, and a friend or acquaintance shakes you awake. Soon after, you start dozing again and veering off a cliff. The person loudly yells at you to wake up because the tires are meeting gravel and grass—not a good sign.

Will you be mad because they screamed and hurt your feelings while probably letting out a couple of expletives, or be mature and thank them for stopping a fatal accident? The rebuke may have stung your pride a bit, but it also saved two lives. Why get upset when someone lovingly corrects an error in our life? Wouldn't you rather receive wise corrective advice from a friend than a *frenemy* (enemy cloaked as a friend)? Don't be afraid to speak or receive truth in love because truth is currency.

Truth is Your Calling Card

The truth is worth its weight in gold. It may cost you an acquaintance (notice I didn't say friend) or two, a job, or a close relationship, but it is more valuable than them all. A person can take away material possessions, fame, and power, but they can't take away truth—it remains even when suffocated and beaten down. It will stand the test of time, unlike perishable possessions. It's like your driver's license, passport, or military identification—people can identify you by it.

You may be familiar with the phrase, "Your word is your bond." Truer words could not be spoken, pun intended! Truthful or untruthful communication precedes your presence, doesn't it? When someone mentions a company's name, you probably begin to think about the quality of their product or service.

For instance, you *might* think more highly of a luxury automobile brand like Mercedes-Benz versus Kia. These are just examples. I'm not passing judgment on these vehicles' value or worthiness. I personally haven't owned either brand. I'm more of a Saab woman—I wish they were still in production today.

Back to the topic. Mercedes-Benz might be viewed more favorably because it has built a reputation for producing fine automobiles since 1926 and has exceptional customer service to enforce that image. A Mercedes-Benz doesn't have to be present; it is just the name, and you have instantly formulated an opinion. Like many corporations, Mercedes-Benz has worked hard to protect the integrity of its products.

They control the public's thoughts by creating pitch-perfect advertisements and producing quality automobiles and transportation solutions. Did you catch that? You and I can control (for the most part) how others perceive us, but our actions are paramount to that perception.

It's the same concept concerning our credibility and our trustworthiness. You build a reputation—good or bad—and it follows you in every realm of life, personal and professional. This is why parents should stress the importance of a good reputation early in their child's life. Waiting until they are teenagers is, in my opinion, far too late.

Truth remains even when beaten down and suffocated--it lives to tell the story.

You'd better believe students already have a reputation for being good, academic, well-behaved pupils, a bump on the log that takes up space, or undesirable trouble-making hooligans. This is practical living, folks.

For example, your name speaks volumes to automobile dealers who check your credit score "before you sign on the dotted line at the dealership or to the bank before you close on that dream home you've been sacrificing for by eating

Ramen noodles to afford it. The bottom line is that your name carries weight—albeit positive or negative. We determine which one we'll be known for, not a gossip, hater, or life-long adversary. Guard your name by speaking the truth.

When someone mentions my or your name, they should have pleasant thoughts. Hopefully, we will see how important truth is. People know you as someone they can trust or one they laugh at/with only. Can you be counted on to speak the truth?

H – helpful

"Do not let any unwholesome talk come out of your mouths, but only what helps build others up according to their needs, that it may benefit those who listen."
Ephesians 4:29 (NIV)

What does it mean to be helpful in your communication—serving and assisting (Merriam Webster, 2024). A helpful person makes it easier to do a job, deal with a problem, and is willing to assist others. When you help someone, you make a task, situation, or matter more manageable and pleasant for them to handle or complete. You are there to render aid in whatever desired capacity. There are professional "helpful communicators" such as spiritual leaders, therapists, psychiatrists, motivational speakers, psychologists, and mentors who guide us through life. And then there's you and me. Although we don't have a degree, we can also be helpful by effectively communicating. To be effective communicators, our words should move a person or group closer to finding a solution(s), not creating more issues.

Watch your mouth! Grown folks don't have time for empty talk.

How many times have you needed a problem solved, only for an "adviser" to give you everything but sound advice? If you're like me, you probably wish they had just remained silent. Their counsel was not wise at all, and it turned out to be the wrong guidance. Just as a person dying of thirst doesn't need directions to a clothing store, neither should we dispense irrelevant information.

Information must add value to a person's being, not detract from or cloud an already unclear situation. We're constantly growing, and that growth should lead us to analyze the benefits and necessity of our words. Are we talking just to be talking or doing so with a productive end goal?

Make it Count

As you grow and mature, you realize you don't have time for empty talk, only helpful conversation. Empty talk stems from an empty word. An empty word serves only a grammatical function without adding meaning. For example, if you ask a person if they filled their car up with gas, "up" adds nothing of significance. You could have inquired whether the individual filled their car with gas, which would suffice. Empty talk, then, is stringing words together with no purpose. We all do it, and I regularly monitor my speech and writing because I have a slight problem with run-on sentences, fast cadence words, and veering off into leftfield.

Empty talk lacks any intended outcome or goal; it's just saying something for the sake of speaking. Empty talk means nothing; the person is just talking to combat silence, boredom, nervousness, or other emotions. I have nothing against small talk; I feel there should be a return—even at awkward office parties. Let's not pretend we haven't attended one, two, or three.

I had more than my share when I was active-duty military. People who barely say hello to each other at work (for various reasons: jealousy, spite, racism, income) are now forced to talk and hold conversations. Inevitably, the chat leads to either the weather, sports, family, or your hometown. If you're going to talk, at least learn something about the individual because talking for the heck of it is pointless—it's empty!

No Substance

Empty talk uses filler words to compensate for the lack of substantive thoughts and conversation. Although empty words have no value, they still have power. Words have the authority and ability to change the atmosphere they enter. The atmosphere at several of my Air Force assignments often made me dread going to work. The sheer amount of foolery was quite sad, and usually, there was swift retribution if you weren't a "team player" in the shenanigans.

When I didn't join in the gossip sessions describing who was getting kicked out because they were having sex with so and so's spouse, I became their next unlucky target. I was not fond of those offices because I knew bitter people were waiting to spew negative, cruel, non-productive conversations all day.

Some working environments became hostile and unbearable because their words hovered like dark clouds. Visitors came and went quickly lest they pick up an infection from the unhealthy setting. You've also been there and done that, right? I'm sure you've experienced something similar in your career/profession.

Based solely on the examples listed, there are good reasons why our words should be measured and calculated. We all must grow into this knowledge. It doesn't happen overnight. Remember, time and experience are our teachers.

As an experienced baker knows, baking a cake requires specific ingredients that should be included to ensure maximum taste and texture. Certain ingredients "help" make the cake edible and delectable. Our words should do the same. Helpful ideas and words make conversing easier "to take" for both parties.

If you add extra fixings and higher amounts of the sweetened mix, chances are it won't turn out just right—something will be off, amiss. Again, it is the same with our words. You and l adding untested fixings (words) to a conversation is a recipe for disaster. Just as you have no clue how the cake will turn out when you add unknown components, you don't know the possible results of speaking with unknown variables either. The result could be harmful or helpful.

Helpful communication
brings clarity to the receiver.

Helping...

Our words ought to HELP—render relief or assist. If you have information that can help and choose not to share it, that's selfish. You're preventing someone from finding an answer to their problem. There is a legal term, obstruction of justice, whereby an individual can be legally culpable for not disclosing valuable details concerning an ongoing investigation.

A person can be arrested for keeping relevant information away from proper authorities because what they have can unlock puzzle pieces and shed light on a case. You're guilty of communication obstruction when you can help but don't. Helpful words add value and remove obstacles attached to problems. Stop obstructing! Many of us have been guilty in the past and still are of withholding—time for a scenario.

Scenario

A stranger, new to your city, asks you for directions to a business across town, and you, feeling impatient and cranky, give them extended directions instead of a shortcut. Also, instead of telling them the store was closed that day, you allowed them to drive 10 or 20 miles one-way, knowing the establishment wasn't open. That individual wasted gas and precious time better utilized heading to their final destination on the right day. You, the speaker, had the opportunity to bring clarity to an individual needing HELP but did the opposite.

Clarity is a by-product of supportive communication whereby the receiver receives something beneficial. By being helpful, you make clear what was once murky. If your words are not performing this function, you are not helping. It's as simple as that—we know when we're being unhelpful. Let's not be coy. You had/have the power to help someone but won't due to jealousy, anger, revenge, bitterness, or straight-up pettiness. I could keep going on, but I think you get it. Your decision to withhold needed information places(d) another at a disadvantage. I know, and you probably know, some misguided souls who think it's hip, edgy, and fun to conceal data that would otherwise be contributive. If you are or have been one of these people, realize it does nothing for your personal growth.

> You are guilty of
> communication obstruction
> when you can help and
> decide not to!

You may derive some sick, sadistic pleasure from making someone's day go awry. What you don't realize is it causes you harm. The damage occurs when you reap what you've sown. This goes beyond the golden rule of *do unto others as you would have them do unto you*. The golden rule sounds nice in theory, but what about in practice? Would you want an individual with no moral compass doing unto you? I think not. Drugs, physical abuse, and prejudice may be okay for them, so they'll have no problem being on the receiving end of toxic behaviors as well as doling them out.

Unlike the golden rule, the sowing and reaping concept is impartial and not predicated on fickle emotions or hidden agendas. Both faith believers and nonreligious individuals are likely familiar with oft-quoted Galatians 6:10 (American Standard Version), "*Be not deceived, whatsoever a man soweth, that shall he also reap.*" We will discuss this fully later in another chapter, but we'll touch the surface for now. The above scripture says you can't do anything you want to people and expect not to receive compensation. Treat others kindly in word and deed, and it will return to you.

I'LL HELP YOU; I'LL HELP YOU NOT?

I'm reminded of when I was stationed overseas in the early 1990s. My assignment was ending, and I had to prepare (it's called "out-processing" in military terminology) to leave for another overseas location. Mind you, I was still relatively new to the armed forces, having joined the Air Force a couple of years earlier. Yes, dear reader, there is a reason I am giving you this background.

No more pettiness--don't withhold information to exact revenge!

During this time, I found myself at the military transportation office to make my travel arrangements back to the United States and then on to the new overseas duty assignment. A sergeant I knew worked there, and I didn't think he was salty until after I left that base. I previously met him while running mail errands for my squadron, and on one occasion, he stopped me and asked if I wanted to go out with him on a date. I politely told him I wasn't interested.

When I walked through the door, he smirked. After hearing I was there to out-process, he proceeded to "help" me with my travel plans and reservations. He asked for a copy of my PCS (permanent change of station) orders, an authorization form stating I have permission to leave one base for another. The travel document indicated my destination, and he informed me there were several routes to my new destination. I asked which was the fastest and least complicated, and he answered and booked the flights for me. Mission accomplished, yes? NO!!

Once I arrived at the connecting military terminal in the new country, I gave them my travel itinerary to obtain tickets for boarding the train to my new duty station. The sergeant behind the desk looked at me as if I was crazy. He told me there was no train to take me to my next assignment. He then explained that I would ride for about three days if I took a train. Now I am bewildered because Mr. Married "when I'm state-side but single everywhere else" said it was a 2-hour train ride. Since traveling by train for three days was out of the question, they had to find me a flight to this location, which was at the southern tip of the country, and I, at the time, was at the very northern.

Days later, when I finally arrived at the host nation's military airport, my section supervisor quipped that it was the oddest thing he'd seen in his 15 years of being stationed there. No American military ever came through a military charter flight to that airport; they all flew commercial!

What's the point of this story, you ask? He withheld pertinent information that he knew would hamper my travel and purposely miscommunicated to exact some petty revenge for a perceived slight. The reality is I didn't and would have never entered a relationship with him, even if he was single. Coincidentally, he didn't reveal to me (and probably didn't to other women) that he was married when he asked me on a date. I only found out afterward because I was friendly with some ladies who worked in the base personnel office.

Integrity bothers those with evil intentions.

I can only surmise this guy was used to getting his way and used his position to co-opt sexual favors from young, unsuspecting female airmen and was astonished that I wouldn't accommodate his advances. Simply put, his pride and ego were wounded, and he lashed out. Had I been a little more seasoned (this was my first duty station), I would have checked my tickets and inquired about my itinerary before leaving the base. It would ensure I was going to the right place with expedience, not taking a Greyhound bus route via military aircraft. There's no reason to 'help' someone when you know you're not helping. We need to GROW UP in a hurry.

IF YOU'RE NOT HELPING, YOU'RE NOT HELPING!

This chapter's foundational scripture comes from the fourth book of Ephesians, verse 29 (Ephesians 4:29). The first part warns us not to let unwholesome talk leave our mouths. We do have control over what we say. No one can make you say anything you don't want to. They can influence you by their words or body posture, but they don't have the power to coerce you unless by gunpoint or other equally dubious means. Don't give others the power to force your hand. Or shall I say force your mouth to say things you'll regret later?

It doesn't matter what the circumstances are. I do say that lightly, but it still stands. You and I both know friends and family who have suffered traumatic events by way of a ruthless victimizer. Even with such abuse, it doesn't give the victim the right to abuse others in turn. So, it is with our words. We may have had nasty encounters with those who tried to belittle or humiliate us, but we don't have to repay them or others in kind. Of course, do leave and find safety if you find yourself in dangerous, life-threatening circumstances. But do not get caught up in the drama. Abrasive and demeaning words are futile and unhelpful. They serve neither the speaker nor the receiver.

The second part of that verse says, *"only that which is helpful for building others up based on their needs."* Notice the "only" piece? I should be voicing words that WILL enhance and develop. Too often, we do the opposite and employ *unhelpful* words like a wartime missile destroying enemy territory. I won't get on my soapbox (too much) about the lack of civility in today's society.

I must say there is a general disregard for humanity, a type of malicious detachment. A detachment born of difficult childhoods and distrust of life itself has otherwise decent people doing and saying the most outlandish things. Words spoken in secret and behind closed doors are now blasted on the big screen, news, and even in the school system because times have changed, they say. I somewhat agree with that statement. We are in a different era; however, it doesn't give you the right to be cold and hard towards the world or innocent people who didn't cause your pain.

We don't act that way, right? Determine in your heart and mind today not to tear people down with your words. After you've dragged them/set them straight/or read them, what have you accomplished? I'll answer, NOTHING! You got it out of your mind and off the chest—what now?

NOTE: I hate that I have to clarify, but I am not saying there are no (zero) cases where you don't have to address pressing issues or problems. Wisdom dictates otherwise. Some things must be set straight because they affect your livelihood, safety, reputation, and health. It's time for another scenario.

SCENARIO

Imagine experiencing this in your professional life. You have a colleague who also attends the same church and shares some acquaintances. That person is absent on a staff meeting day when the commander points out that she needs to improve her customer service skills.

Later that day, you pull the person aside and encourage them to step up their customer care game. Unbeknownst to you, she secretly dislikes you and confronts the commander the next day when you are out of the office performing administrative duties. Another person happens to be in that meeting and pulls you aside when you return. You are shocked to hear the colleague asked the commander about his comments regarding her demeanor. The drama, right?

Feeling a little hot under the collar, you go to her office and ask her why she betrayed your confidence and goodwill gesture. She flippantly says she doesn't care, and if somebody says something about her, she will challenge them. How would you handle this situation?

This is a true story, and I will explain how I handled it. After informing my co-worker that she couldn't be trusted and that I'd never help her again, to which she didn't seem to care, I marched my scared self to my old-school security police commander's office. Thankfully, he was alone and working on some weekly reports. I explained that I told my co-worker what was said in the staff meeting out of concern for her professionalism and career. Grinning, he removed his thick horned-rim glasses and told me I had learned a valuable lesson about people and trust, and there were those who didn't want help, and sticking my neck out for them was reckless—it was duly noted.

I had to take that thrashing. I apologized for speaking out of turn and shamedly returned to my office. Hindsight being 20/20, I would've kept the conversation surrounding her nasty attitude and lack of customer service skills to myself and picked up on the cleverly hidden signs that Ms. Mean Girl hated my guts. Later, after this incident, I was informed of some disparaging comments she made about me to another.

My point is that had I not set the record straight by humbling myself and apologizing to my commander, I would have more than likely received a lower performance report rating from him, and I would've been guessing if it was that incident or his belief I didn't deserve an exceptional evaluation. Although he disagreed with my divulging a critique shared with his senior staff, he surprisingly understood why. By the way, I received the highest marks possible from him during my subsequent evaluation and a commendation medal to boot. Take that, Ms. Hater!

I hope that scenario was reassuring. Integrity wins in the end. Our words, speech, and communication can ruin a livelihood. Life is all about choices. You and I choose whether to help or hurt others every day. What do you decide?

Choose Strategy

The goal is no more "talking to be talking." Yes, there are times when spontaneous dialogue occurs, but even in that, there is direction. We want to be strategic in every area of our lives, especially speaking. I get it; talking is fun, especially when it requires little thought or accountability.

As I get older, as I am sure is the case for most reaching the half-a-century marker, you want to make every second count, and spending an hour or two just prattling seems wasteful. Let's avoid what I like to call the three "non's" which are communication hurdles we ALL have struggled with. These three overlapping deterrents will hinder or stop efficient communication:

1. **Non-productive talk**- is talking with no goal in mind. Unfortunately, most conversations fall into this category. As stated earlier, there is nothing wrong with casual communication (also known as small talk). We all do it, and it serves a purpose. However, even casual chit-chat can be purposeful with intentional focus. A simple "Hello, you look beautiful today" can be used as a greeting and a word of cheer. What could've been another common expression now serves a greater purpose of building another's confidence.

2. **Nonsense talk**- is a conversation with no rhyme or reason; this talk has no meaning. I rank this as the second most frustrating hurdle. Remember the time(s) you've been talking to a person, and you felt it was a colossal waste of time? Not just because it didn't interest you but because it didn't make sense. I'm

referring to those who oversaturate themselves in foolishness, like watching and re-hashing trash television or discussing the latest celebrity hookup (unless it's your job and income is received). Their lives are spent regurgitating data that I call non-nutritive. Like soda pop, it might taste good but lacks vitamins or minerals. Nonsense doesn't build or exhort. It does not push you into greater or propel you toward destiny. What, then, is the use?

3. **Non-communicative talk**- is an unwillingness to talk or share information. Remember the example of the stranger asking for directions to a place of business only to be sidetracked and given little to no assistance? A non-communicative person can help, but they don't. Imagine sitting in an important business meeting where everyone is brainstorming, and one person has the solution but sits there in silence, knowing they hold the missing piece. Would you not be furious with that person? They can help but do not out of pride or plain old spite.

The list above is straightforward. When you talk nonsense, are non-communicative, and have non-productive conversations, it's a telltale sign that you're not ready to do the work and advance to the next leg of your journey. One thing grade school, elementary, or primary school teachers (depending on your regional upbringing) look for in their students is aptitude mastery commensurate with grade level.

If a student doesn't understand the course material or has limited comprehension, they will recommend the child repeat that grade or attend summer school. Do you have the skill set to graduate and advance? It's that next-level living standard, remember? Go back to the preface and introduction if you need a reminder. Advancement happens when YOU are ready to proceed. Are you ready, or is remedial training needed?

 ## WHAT'S THE LESSON?

Hopefully, this chapter has given you an in-depth understanding of helpful communication. Please pause and take inventory of your life. Stop and reflect. Can you say you are helpful? Ask a family member or reliable friend for input if you're unsure. Trust me, they won't hesitate to tell you—in fact, they might be a little too honest.

How do we perform this assessment? Be introspective. We take stock of our conversation and what comes out of our mouth because it (the mouth) can and will make declarations and decrees the owner has no intention of keeping or honoring--promises we knew we'd never fulfill. However, our actions don't lie. You can tell someone you will help them all day, but if no support is rendered, you haven't helped. While we're on this, helping someone is more than mere words. Action and follow-up need to be taken if necessary—enough of this sending "well wishes and happy thoughts" when someone is in dire straits. Being supportive involves both words and actions.

If you feel you are missing the mark in "helpfulness," you probably need to step back and search your heart and mind. What is holding you back from being helpful in speech and deed? Maybe something in the past. You were once pleasant and eager to assist, but someone took advantage. Now, you vow to take care of yourself only. Please understand that I'm not condemning you.

We all have something to "work on" and periodically fall short. It's not that we want to be habitual "fallers," but life happens, and we need to regroup, dust ourselves off, and get back up. There's no need to wallow in self-pity—it produces nothing. We can acknowledge our shortcomings, deal with them, and move on.

I want to fortify your spirit. If you know you haven't been authentic or helpful in the past, it doesn't matter. There's not a person born who hasn't experienced regret for what could've been. Nevertheless, carrying sorrow for a life you'll never live isn't productive. Cry your last cry and dry those tears.

*Leave your past in the past--
it is dead. Concentrate on
the here and now.*

I have to get a little preachy here, but I feel led to tell you to let go. Holding onto the hurt closes you off from receiving more. That pain is like a closed fist. Nothing new can be placed there until you release those fingers and open your palm. Do you know how much you can be missing out on? I'm not minimizing any trauma you've experienced—I just know it's not sustainable.

You're too good a person to stay at that address. You've got to pack your bags and leave. Nothing will be delivered there except more pain and disappointment. The past has passed; make peace with it, leave it behind. You are charting a new and different path that will lead you to purpose and destiny—a path where your speech is seasoned with the right words—genuine and helpful words.

After you've read this book and applied the concepts, your speech will add another instrument to your burgeoning tool chest. All artisans use different tools to perform their jobs. A doctor has a stethoscope and reflex hammer; a hair stylist uses various combs, rollers, and scissors; and a mechanic has a plethora of pliers, wrenches, and screwdrivers.

The point is that you need different tools to handle various situations. Therefore, there are several tools to the THINK process at your disposal. You must be true, helpful, inspiring, speak when necessary, and kind. They work together in tandem. The words you and I say should ADD substance, not subtract from one's life, just like a toolbox enhances and facilitates a skilled craftsman's work.

Are you improving another's existence or diminishing it? Don't know which category you fall into? Ask and answer these questions. HINT—Affirmatives mean you are on the right track:

- Will the words about to tumble out of my mouth be helpful? You already know before you say them if they will be useful. Don't allow your emotions to run wild—pause before you hit play.

- Do they positively impact the intended individual? Words will impact a living, breathing human with feelings on the receiving end. You, as the sender, can speak forth, good or bad.

It's now time to THINK! Whenever you participate in a conversation, you should consider the usefulness of your input before putting it out into the world. We either help or we don't. Which will you do?

I – inspiring

"Anxiety in a man's heart weighs it down, But a good (encouraging) word makes it glad."
Proverbs 12:25 (AMP)

So far, we've learned that our words need to be true and helpful, and now it's time to inspire. We should ponder if our words are inspirational BEFORE adding our two cents to the conversation. The value of our ill-spoken 2¢ declines quicker than the latest must-have cell phone, which will be replaced in six months. When we interject dreary and self-defeating talk, we aren't inspiring. Seeing enough negativity generated by life experience, I can't imagine why we'd want to fill our spirits with rubbish. We don't need vain, empty talk. We need fruitful words that produce after its kind. Let's inspire!

ARE YOU INSPIRATIONAL?

The simple definition of inspiring is *causing people to want to do or create something or lead better lives.* (Merriam Webster, 2024) Our conversation ought to stir, engage, promote, and encourage the receiver to live life abundantly. In short, our voice should be one of hope and expectancy.

Inspiring others through our speech comes from a place of wholeness.

    An inspirational person seeks to draw or bring out the best qualities in a person, even when the receiver doesn't want the same thing or is not receptive to change. Fond memories of a first-grade teacher gently coaxing you to sound out a word in a sentence might come to mind. You were happy with "dog and cat," but your teacher knew there was more to explore.

    Inspiring someone is as simple as saying, "I believe in you," or "You can do it." Negative or positive words have power, and inspiring someone is just as easy as discouraging them. It doesn't take extra effort to uplift and encourage one another. When we talk, it doesn't cost us more brain cells or breath to support our neighbor, a stranger, or a friend. Inspiring others means our words should have an elevating quality. So, how can we be inspirational?

Correct and Inspire?

One way we can be inspirational, which is not often discussed, is by correcting errors. Stay with me; I haven't lost it! Correcting an error can be a powerful tool when done correctly. Although it can be uncomfortable and unpleasant (to both receiver and sender) when it occurs, it still serves the same goal of inspiration.

Parents inspire their children when they put them in time-out or render another form of "constructive" reinforcement, also known as discipline (i.e., taking away privileges or extra chores). Maybe your child said something distasteful or lied. You know this is not the behavior you want to be exhibited or normalized, so you convey your disappointment and appropriately chastise him/her. You do this to motivate them to be and do better. It was an unpleasant task, but it had to be done.

The corrective measures were taken because you know the child has great potential and want the best for him/her. You are working to bring out those hidden qualities that often come out only through adversity, mentoring, or self-awareness. This corrective discipline is intentional and positioned as a learning tool and life lesson—not abuse!

Abuse is when you act out of anger, fear, or some other negative emotion, causing harm to another person. That harm could be physical or psychological. I would never advocate abuse on another human being—let's make that clear, especially physical. The only time your hands should be used to inflict harm is in self-defense because your very life may depend on it. One more time: self-defense ➔ yes, abuse ➔ no. You don't inspire someone by battering.

Inspiring individuals through our speech comes from a place of wholeness within ourselves, not a fabricated outward presentation. If you don't possess a quality, how can you exhibit that quality? I know there's the nature vs. nurture debate, but I believe that if a skill, talent, gift, or ability isn't housed in you (dormant or active), it won't emerge.

You can fake it for so long before it becomes obvious you don't have the necessary competency. I'm also talking to you job seekers—creating and submitting a resume full of lies. Come on, folks. Your boss will figure out that you don't type 100 words per minute when it takes you all day to finish a two-page report. And that foreign language spin won't work when you're promoted to lead the international sales team and don't know how to greet the exchange staff in their native tongue. My my my, what shall we do? BE HONEST.

Uninspiring folk do not inspire because their inspiration is depleted!

I don't have the skills to be a world-class singer. That talent or gift just isn't there. I can take singing lessons for 30 years to no avail. The idiom, "you can't squeeze blood out of a turnip," is very apropos. People who struggle to inspire usually don't feel inspired themselves. How, then, can you inspire if you don't feel it? Find yourself.

Find Your Purpose, Become an Inspiration

Finding yourself means knowing and acting on your life's purpose. Purpose is the reason something exists, an intended or desired result[2]. Our existence is why we are living and gracing others with our presence. Do you know why God placed you here? If you do, that's wonderful. If you don't, it's time to find out. What are some ways to discover your purpose and figure out life? Mind you, this is a book written with spiritual values. Therefore, I will be giving you spiritual and practical means. They are as follows:

1. **Dreams** – Joseph, the famed biblical character who owned the coat of many colors, was around 17 when he had a dream. It was a dream foretelling his royal status. The vision gave prophetic insight as to who and what he'd become. Don't dismiss your dreams just because you think they're random. They might hold the key to your next business venture, future spouse, or witty invention.

2. **Prophetic Vessels** – Prophetic vessels can be a person in the prophetic office, a person with the gift of prophecy, or someone God uses for a time. Truly prophetic individuals spiritually see things about you (not something made up or said for material gain and fame), especially your purpose. I experienced this myself while stationed in Asia. A person spoke some words into my life about my purpose and destiny that seemed ridiculous but are now starting to emerge some 20 years later.

3. **Word of God** – I can't begin to tell you the number of times I've been at a standstill and didn't know what direction or move to make. Feeling frustrated, I "happened" to pick up the Bible and "find" a scripture relating to my challenge. You can read scripture, and a person or occupation stands out and begins to come alive and resonate. A passion for research ensues. Before you know it, that love grows to the point you're consumed (I mean that in a healthy manner). Lo and behold, you've stumbled upon your purpose. Am I saying it will be that easy? No. However, it's a start in the right direction.

4. **Mentor/Trusted Advisor** – Those closest to us—friends, mentors, or advisors—know our strengths and weaknesses. You might think you are very talented in an area, but they can ascertain that's not for

you. For example, you're meant to own a home cleaning service, but because it isn't seen as glamorous or profitable, you try to find another purpose that suits your idea of who you are—fail! You are invigorated when you clean. You feel at one with the cleaning instruments and products. Your skills, gifts, talents, and abilities point to the cleaning service: attention to detail, spatial foresight, and structure. Yet you want to be a reality star. That mentor will lovingly tell you to re-think because they see your passion and zeal for cleaning and know you will waste precious time and resources you'll never get back while pursuing a temporary high instead of purpose.

You will inspire others with words, knowing who you are, and walking decisively. As I mentioned earlier, there's more to thinking before you speak; it's also about works. You show people you love them by what you say AND do. We think before we speak and allow the correct action(s) to follow. It would be best if you weren't motivating, then do an about-face and act foolishly. It's like giving a rousing speech and then immediately cussing everyone out. Can we say Twilight Zone? If we're going to be inspirational, let's be inspirational, not straddling the fence because someone's life depends on our words.

A BREATH OF FRESH AIR

Have you ever noticed how most inspirational speakers are a joy to be around? You feel revived and, for lack of a better word—inspired. Why is that? Inspirational people know their purpose and feel comfortable in their skin. Inspirational—not giving pep talks or being nice. The true essence of inspiration is breathing life into another person's spirit.

When you inspire through speech, you are pushing life toward them. For illustrative purposes, I'll use a farmer. The farmer knows he/she can till the soil and amend it with fertilizer, but there's no harvest unless they water the plant, crop, or seed. The water stimulates and is essential for the plant to grow.

To inspire is to water dead places in someone else's journey. You and I pass dead people every day (while shopping, on the street, at our job, in church) who've given up. Perhaps you spoke to them and thought they were having a bad day; the truth is they are having a bad life. They checked out ages ago and are here in the flesh, but their spirit died.

Inspiration is the water that saturates someone's parched dream, vision, and hope.

In fact, there's a tombstone with their name, birth date, and an 'I gave up' date. Will you take time out of your already busy schedule to replenish and lift a bowed down head, or be the wind beneath their broken wings? Or are you too downtrodden and busy yourself?

You might be saying about now, "Pamela, I didn't sign up for all of this extra material. I'm only here for the T-H-I-N-K acronym. I don't need this heavy stuff." My friend, this is a part of it. Either we embrace and get on board the next stop to "Excellent Living" or stay in "Mediocre Ville," which is next door to "Stagnation Town." I'm ready to do what it takes to excel. Let's do this together because you have something on the inside that can stir and energize one in need.

You are the Rain

You don't need a degree, backing from an influential person, or experience to motivate. Are we going to follow 1 Thessalonians 5:11 by encouraging and comforting one another and building our fellow human beings? Encouragement leads to comfort, and comfort leads to growth. Whether you are a comforter, builder, or one who cheers, you will inspire.

Water in a desert is more
precious than gold.

Countless people are parched in a desert and desperately need inspiration sprinkled liberally—don't be stingy. If you've ever walked through one, you'll know how isolated and barren they are. One may be afraid to reach out, and we can extend that life-saving branch, thus pulling them to well-being. They may feel dead, but you can help bring them back with your words. Job 14:7 tells us that a tree will bud and put out branches like a young plant at the scent of water.

Think back to when you had a problem and sought help. Just the thought of you going to seek help made you feel better. You were yet to speak with them, but the idea was enough to lift a heavy burden from your weary shoulders. Now imagine a downtrodden person severely inspirationally deprived, receiving overdue sustenance and revived because of a spoken word. Get that, a spoken word!

A person on the brink of suicide could be saved by a positive word spoken at the right moment. A husband about to leave his three children and wife needs to hear a motivating word before he potentially destroys five lives. A bullied teen needs to know it gets better before he shoots up a school and kills himself. Somebody needs hope, and you are that hope. You are the water quenching the thirstiness of their dry spell. Do we not grasp how vital it is to inspire?

WHAT'S THE LESSON?

Your words, will they inspire someone to move forward in life, to build character? Will they be grateful you crossed their path or wish they'd never met you because your words brought death? Instead of energizing them, they felt depleted after being in your presence. Proverbs 12: 25 says, *"Anxiety in a man's heart weighs it down, but a good (encouraging) word makes it glad."* Do you want to inspire? Bring an encouraging word, one that will give hope, joy, and affirmation, not heaviness.

The first part of verse 25 is not a shocker: anxiety will wear you out mentally and physically. Daily uncertainties and stress contribute to worry. Stress brings you down to a place of uncertainty and fear. Everyone experiences stress regardless of gender, ethnicity, or socioeconomic status. Don't think for a second your heart won't sink when trouble knocks on your door. I've had several deaths in my family since first publishing this book, and let me tell you, there were times I couldn't see my way out. It takes time to bounce back.

Maybe your heart is already weighed down. What burden are you grappling with today that makes you need a comforting word? Perhaps it's not great news from your doctor. A child is acting up in school. You can't pay your rent/mortgage. These scenarios would bring us to a place of despair if left unchecked. But a life-giving word can counter despair and provide hope—this is why we inspire!

I'm hoping this is a good word for you, dear reader. You ought to feel motivated while reading and ultimately finish this book. Why? My goal is to inspire you to reach that level of greatness by thinking before you speak. Is there a stirring in you, a reignited desire to be inspirational?

N – necessary

"Anyone who guards his words protects his life; anyone who talks too much is ruined."
Proverbs 13:3 (ISV)

Do we need to say anything else here? However, for the sake of continuity, let's recap the standard definition. Necessary is the state of being inescapable or required (Merriam-Webster.com, 2024). Recollect the moment you spoke something and, in hindsight, realize it wasn't even needed. As soon as it came out, you knew it was messed up. Those around you might have *thought* you were more intelligent and wiser, but a slip of the tongue told them otherwise. Proverbs 17:28 hilariously says, *"Even fools who keep quiet are thought to be wise; as long as they keep their mouths shut, they're smart."* Who would've thought pondering and carefully selecting our words had such an advantage? Like wearing glasses, staying silent can create the illusion of intelligence and wisdom. It's not until we indiscriminately flap our gums that we are found out.

Scenario

Dressed to impress, you roll up to your 20th high school reunion. Memories of being picked on and snickered at for low grades, you are now ready to show off. You purchased a For Dummies book on world geography and want to put your sworn enemies in their place with all your wisdom and knowledge. Although you briefly skimmed the pages, you know you are ready for primetime. You're not, and no one would've known you were clueless at your reunion dance until you blurted out that you were learning African. There's no such language as "African."

You are referring to one of the 54 separate countries comprising the motherland like it's the whole continent. A quick Google search will inform your classmates that some 2,000 languages are spoken, and you don't know which one you've memorized for this exact moment. Not a good look, eh? Your quest to look smart has backfired.

What seems like an eternity is an agonizing thirty seconds of silence, and you want the gym floor to open up and swallow you. It was good that the cameras were not rolling to catch your tightening, red, embarrassed face and everyone else's perplexed expression. It would help if you had exercised caution like a blinking yellow light at a 4-way stop. Instead of proceeding slowly, you barreled through and caused an accident (an embarrassing one, I might add). Had wisdom prevailed, you would've looked in all directions, then accelerated, saving face.

Don't Barrel Through

Now, apply this to your communication skills. Are you a wise communicator or uncaring and bullish--you speak with abandon, wreaking havoc and dealing with hurt feelings and damaged relationships later. Prudence says to contemplate before you let them escape (words, that is). Genuinely think it through the first time because you might not get a second chance to rectify your speech or actions.

Like fine china, once words break something, the damage can be mended, but the cracks will still show when you put the pieces together using cheap and ineffective glue. That cup, if stressed enough, could break again. It will be sensitive in the places it sustained damage. I know several people in relationships like that piece of fractured porcelain. One event, one comment, and they're cracking again.

An unchecked mouth can lead to your teeth checking out too!

We understand how important it is to watch our words and preserve relationships. If we don't, devastation is often the result. Be careful! Proverbs 13:3 warns, "Anyone who guards his words protects his life; anyone who talks too much is ruined." Exercise discretion to protect your reputation, physical body, relationships, and mind.

Go back in time with me, back to elementary, junior high, and high school. You'll remember a student (or it could've been you) known for talking entirely too much. They had a habit of inserting themselves into places and conversations uninvited. All that talk landed them in hot water several times, one fight after another. You'd think they learned their lesson after the first beatdown, but unfortunately, they did not.

It was the same occurrence: open a big mouth and get hit in the big mouth. It seemed like nothing could deter them. Either they grew out of their messy ways, or eventually, a fight came that they couldn't bounce back from—one that changed them forever. Sad, but we must learn we can't and shouldn't say whatever we feel. Proverbs chapter 13 and verse 3 is trying to save millions from getting their hair pulled from the root, eyes blacked, and teeth loosened or knocked out.

Was there ever a time when we wondered whether allowing our lips to move faster than Mario Andretti on a racetrack was necessary? Diarrhea of the mouth, one that is always running, ensures you'll be joining the ranks of those in "Regret Land." It's where you'll reside if you don't organize those thoughts and control that tongue, a small but mighty organ. Talk about a body part with the power to inflict more hurt than two fists and kick you further down than a martial artist. It's high time we become wisdom-minded.

Move away from *"Regret Land."* Nothing but regret lives there.

May You Find Wisdom

Proverbs 21:23 says, *"Keep your mouth closed, and you'll stay out of trouble."* That was a strong admonishment. A big chunk of our problems would be solved if we followed this advice: zipped our lips, shut up, kept mum, held our mule (that's an old one)—use whatever euphemism pleases you. The tongue is powerful; mastering it is a sign of great wisdom.

This chapter and verse speak volumes for the big-mouthed student to the local neighborhood gossip. Want to live a long, peaceful, and healthy (read knuckle-free) life? Learn to remain silent unless you have something sound to convey.

An intelligent person will make sure they only speak when needed. Knowing when it's appropriate to talk is just as important as how. Necessary means something is required. Contemplate with me for a minute: is it essential for us to tell a person who just got a speeding ticket not to drive fast?

Not really! I confess I am guilty of doing this. I think it comes from disbelief, but it's completely unnecessary. Chances are incredibly high {sarcasm intended} that they already knew this and were hoping not to get caught, especially if they are habitual speeders.

Your warning will probably be brushed aside. The only thing that will stop (even for a season) a repeat offender is a hefty fine, jail time, loss of license, or a horrific car accident. That's an approachable, uncomplicated example, but what about those instances where a delicate touch is to be used, as in death, legal confinement, or abuse? Do you want to blab and say something untoward about a person's untimely demise, prison sentence, or domestic abuse situation? I certainly wouldn't want to hear something negative during a crisis.

Either say something supportive or close your mouth, friend! I don't mean to be rough, but it needs to be said. "If it ain't necessary, it needs to remain behind your lips." It's not proper English, but it's good advice. Does a situation come to mind where you made comments that were better left unsaid? Your intention was probably harmless, but you got on a roll and said something inappropriate or hurtful.

Learn to remain silent and
speak as wisdom instructs.

How about an individual who compliments someone on their outfit but tells them their shoes don't match? The speaker is unaware that the person only has two pairs of shoes. Ol' Blabbermouth has succeeded in being a jerk and wounding a soul. Try putting yourself in their situation before you speak. Do you like having *your* emotions stomped on and dragged through the mud?

Talking the Hurt Away

Do we think before parting our lips? Constant interjecting and talking too much often points to low self-esteem. Please don't get mad at me now. We're all created differently with unique personalities. Some are stimulated and thrive on interaction, and those who use them to fill a void or make up for a seeming shortcoming. This internal mindset presents outwardly in the following ways:

1. **overly chatty** – This is the life of the party person. Whenever they show up, everyone knows it because they talk non-stop about any and everything. I'm not referencing an outgoing Type A personality who is naturally more sociable (not saying a Type B individual isn't amiable—they are). It's a good thing to be friendly and open to discussion. I'm talking over the top; you'd better notice me or else guys (male and female). They need to be the center of attention, seen and heard, because that's their validation.

2. **abrasive** – This individual is rough around the edges, and they love it. They make a point of being unpleasant, but this is a protective measure to thwart emotional injury. You say hello to them, and they ask why you are greeting them. Seriously, I've had people bite my head off (in church) for saying "hello." Or how about that person who relishes "being real" when the only thing they are is nasty and rude? "Keeping it real" is now code for "I like being nasty, irritable, and am not changing." Honestly, many of us need to reevaluate our whole life.

3. **negative** – "You'd better not try that, you'll fail; don't get married because they'll cheat; be content with where you are (you should to a degree), the world's not the way it was—it's a dangerous place." Those phrases are vocalized by the broken and suspicious. When life handed you lemons, you didn't make lemonade but kept drinking the sour juice. You're easily detected because every other sentence is chock full of pessimism. I strongly urge you to be mindful and not fall into a rut, for it will take a concerted effort to get out. It's easier to run in a ditch than it is to get out of one. Can I get an amen?

4. **braggart** – Bragging can take many forms, but I find using intellect particularly shallow. If showing your smarts is your only way to feel relevant, it's a problem.

In the middle of a random and casual conversation about high gas prices, you bust out the chemical composition of gasoline. Slow down, pal. You have the right information but the wrong time and place. We get it—you scored high on an intelligence test (which, in my opinion, is of questionable value). A set of numbers shouldn't define your worth and respectability. You are more than enough just being you.

Do you fit one of the mindsets? You act hostile so no one can get close to your heart, find negativity where there is none, or boast about what you know. These are signs you need inner healing. You are speaking from a place of insecurity and hurt. A word of insight from Matthew 12:34, "For the mouth speaks out of that which fills the heart" (NASB).

What you allow to leave your mouth reflects what's happening in your heart and mind. If you're in a place of pain, you (and only you) should permit yourself to release every being and experience that scarred and wounded your person. You are not defined by what happened to you in the past. You are who you choose to be now and in the future.

WHAT'S THE LESSON?

Knowing when to talk and or interject takes wisdom and the ability to let others shine (humility). Proverbs 17:27a says, "*The one who knows much says little.*" If you have it (knowledge and wisdom), you don't have to flaunt it because you are secure. You'll have no problem letting others bask in the limelight and won't feel the need to grab attention. You won't be tempted to play the one-upmanship game, which is a sure sign personal growth needs to happen.

It goes like this: one person says something that was received well, so another speaks up and tries to outdo the last comment and get in on the Atta boy/ Atta girl love fest. It's not all about us. Be mature and humble enough to let someone else shine. Don't be the quintessential spoiled brat in a grown-up body. Remember, personal growth is always within reach and a journey worth taking.

Only a selfish child wants to take over and celebrate everyone's birthday like it's theirs. They want the hat and presents too. Mom and Dad must take that self-centered child aside and explain it's not his day and that he will not disrupt the festivities. Like that child, we are to be respectful and wait our turn. I promise your time will come.

🛑 I want to break here and ask you to perform a self-assessment. You can apply this to everything we've discussed so far. Ask yourself these questions, and if you can answer affirmatively, then it's a go. If not, then you had better think twice before talking:

a. What is your motive? Are you trying to help or not? Be honest with yourself.

b. Will it add value to the conversation, situation, or problem?

c. Are you talking just to put your 2 cents in, or do you have a solution?

After taking this assessment, if you believe you've passed, move forward—only when it's appropriate because unnecessary words have gotten many of us in trouble. We need to "read" a situation before diving headfirst. We miss crucial body language and verbal contextual clues when not concentrating and focusing on what should be said. In writing, contextual clues are hints a writer gives to support a reader in defining complicated or unusual words.

We can apply these clues to every area of life, not just reading challenging texts. Verbal clues assist you in understanding a discussion or situation. A first-rate detective, for example, must have impeccable attention to detail. After arriving at a crime scene, their senses take in everything they see, hear, and smell before making a judgment call: foul play or not. What makes us think we can happen upon a chat and start talking when we have no context? It's time for another scenario—yeah!

Not only should you read the room...read the faces.

Scenario

Unbeknownst to you, your popular but shifty co-workers have been in a back corner whispering and talking about robbing a bank after work, and you naively enter the discussion midway and say you want to hang with them after work. You're down for whatever. Without the full details, you almost become an accessory to a crime.

The music is blasting from Jim's brand-new SUV, and you're amazed he can even afford it. The mood is light and cheery, and everyone is laughing and joking. What a great day! You think it's all good until you notice them reach down, pull guns out of a duffle bag inconveniently stashed on the seat next to you, and don Halloween masks. They jump out of the vehicle, run to and open the doors of a local bank.

YOU'RE STUNNED.

Now that the loud radio is turned off, you can hear raised voices and shouting inside. You awake from your stupor, open the cumbersome fancy lock, and hightail it in the opposite direction. In the distance, you hear sirens and an ambulance approaching. Oh my, what did you almost get yourself into?

With burning, rubbery legs and your heart beating a thousand miles a minute, you somehow make it home, a 20-minute journey without losing it. Wild-eyed, you hurriedly place the shaking key in the door lock, barely able to inhale and exhale. Once you can breathe and think coherently, you vow to call your boss the next day and quit, telling him to mail your severance check.

Your next thought is to phone your great aunt, who lives in a one-horse town, and ask her if you can stay a couple of months to get away from it all because you need a change of pace from the hustle and bustle of the big city life—when, in actuality, you're trying to save your life.

What a mess! Somebody should've gotten the complete story before agreeing to a ride-along with part-time criminals. Outlandish scenario? Maybe, but who's to say it hasn't happened? A word of wisdom—observe before you engage. You could save yourself from an appointment with a jail cell or, worse, an undertaker. Learn to listen first, say what's necessary, and move on. We don't have precious time to waste. There's work to do and people to empower!

K – kind

"A soft word turns away anger, and a hard word arouses wrath."
Proverbs 15:1 (ABPE)

The last word in the THINK acronym is kind. But what does it mean to be kind? A kind person has or shows a *gentle nature and a desire to help others, wanting and liking to do good things and to bring happiness to others* (Merriam-Webster, 2024).

Kindness doesn't just happen; it's a deliberate choice, like most things in life. You determine in your mind to be kind. You have to use that small organ, also known as the tongue, to say gracious words because our base mind has little to no inhibition and will spout what it feels like. I remember—funny now, but not then—stories of my nieces and nephews as toddlers. Outings were incredibly fascinating as they'd point and laugh at fellow shoppers in the grocery store who were follicular challenged (bald). Or they loudly ask during church announcements if the older woman in front of our pew was wearing a wig.

Kindness is a deliberate act we CHOOSE to perform every day.

They didn't see a problem because there were no restraints or understanding of the effect of their uncontrollable giggling and forceful declarations. It's been said that children are the most honest speakers, followed by senior citizens. The latter is because they are older and not so concerned with societal repercussions, and the former is because they have no set communication foundation.

Think about it. As a child, you said the first thing that popped into your mind. NO FILTER. If you thought a person was too large, you called them fat. If you thought a person was unattractive, you said that as well. The list goes on and on. It wasn't until a parent, sibling, teacher, or other authority figure told you not to do it that you learned it was inappropriate.

Because it was what? It was unkind. Your training in what was an appropriate/inappropriate word or behavior began. You were now being conditioned to T-H-I-N-K before you speak. As a matter of fact, we knew of this acronym before we "knew" about it.

Whether you live in the western or southern hemisphere, a modern or rustic society, someone taught you manners (to some degree) and acceptable behavior. You were trained to *be* and *do* what is proper per their beliefs and values. You were mainly taught what was "right" and "kind". As we grow psychologically, we further develop our primary teachings or create our own.

This model of kindness—or lack thereof—shapes how we interact today. If you find a person who is very unkind in their demeanor and speech, one or two things have transpired in their life:

1. they were taught to be unkind or

2. life happened, and they've built a protective wall

That wall, in their minds, prevents them from being wounded again. They fail to realize that the same barrier prevents them from receiving the relief they so desperately need or seek.

> The same walls we erect for
> protection are the same
> ones that will imprison us.

Can you imagine calling the ambulance for a sick family member or friend, only to lock the door and refuse to open it when emergency services arrive? That would be an insane and reckless decision, putting the ill person's life at risk.

The same occurs when you authorize baggage (hurt, doubt, envy, and fear) to overrule and cancel out kindness. Want some help? Drop all the baggage preventing you from walking kindly off at the carousel as if you're in an airport and don't pick it up again. There's no charge for extra or oversized ones, either.

Leave it with the experts at the counter who know how to handle it. You guessed it: God is the check-in attendant and knows precisely what to do with your substantial issues. There is no need to ask for a luggage tag or ticket because you're not retrieving those burdens at the end of your journey. Say goodbye there; it weighed you down and impeded your travel.

You're headed for a new destination; the only thing allowed is a carry-on that holds essentials (faith, hope, forgiveness, and love). If you try to retrieve that bag again and sneak anything else into it, you risk being grounded in indifference and lack of sympathy instead of soaring. I may have gotten carried away with that analogy, but I couldn't resist sharing it to encourage you.

I want us to use kindness as a virtue that brings balance and peace to our lives. Kindness is our endless supply of Vitamin B shots. You can inject it daily pain-free, and the receiver has an instant boost of energy and positivity. Kindheartedness is a bridge from despair to hope, death to life, and pandemonium to peace.

KIND WORDS KEEP THE PEACE

Why is kindness so important? Kind words are critical to productive communication. They can diffuse and calm an unstable situation. There it goes again, acknowledging that **you** and **I** have the power and authority to affect change. You might sometimes feel powerless, but you have it within you to bring hope and healing or despair and aggravation. It's the difference between throwing cold water on a fire or juicing it with gasoline.

We choose to extinguish or ignite the fire of unkind words and actions

Do you remember the time you happened upon a heated argument or debate? Each person was slinging unkind words back and forth quicker than Serena Williams' 129 miles per hour serve at the 2013 Australian Open. Neither person wanted to give in and be the voice of reason. In this case, a soft, well-thought-out word/sentence *can* calm the raging storm. I emphasize 'can' because some people refuse to be comforted or reasonable, even when presented with beneficial evidence. These folks like disturbances and wreaking havoc as much as most people like ice cream. He or she sees kindness as frailty, being powerless.

Make no mistake; being kind is not synonymous with weakness. Quite the opposite, being kind in the face of difficulty takes courage. Standing for righteousness is not for the faint at heart because you must be willing to separate your instinctual and dynamic feelings from processed rationale. Our emotions often run high, threatening to lead us, but we have the power to control them and do the mature thing. The immature cop-out is to fly off the handle, fighting with words and action—which solves absolutely nothing and adds new hostility to an already volatile event.

Proverbs 15:1 tells us soft words turn away anger. Don't smirk! This probably seems archaic and foolish in today's fast-moving dog-eat-dog world, where everyone has their guard up and is ready to unload verbally and physically at the first sign of trouble. Every disagreement doesn't require us to hear words so colorful words that would make even a sailor redden. We need balance!

Are You Balancing?

Balance is a meeting in the middle, not on either side of the spectrum. Do you have any fond memories of school recess and the playground? One of my favorite pieces of equipment besides the swing was the seesaw. I loved being in the air, feeling the fresh wind against my face, followed by a speedy drop aided by the other child.

Here is where it could get tricky. If you happened to have a mischievous playmate who abandoned their seat, you might've descended too quickly, resulting in a sore backside. One rascal waited until I got high up, hopped off, and ran away giggling. My poor body paid the price, and I learned a thing or two about giving and not receiving support in return—balance.

Even good things can become bad if misused-- BALANCE is the solution.

Without balance, anything in the universe—good or bad—can become destructive if misused. This is where counterweight comes into play. Take fruit, for instance. Pesticide-free fruit is healthy; however, the United States Department of Agriculture has deemed it wise that eating fruit alone isn't enough to fuel our body, and overconsumption has minimal side effects, albeit still present.

That delicious fruit we love has naturally occurring fructose and sugar. Overeating fruit causes stomach bloat due to our body's inability to absorb significant amounts of fructose. Balancing your diet with grains, proteins, vegetables, and dairy is essential. See how balance works in action?

Kindness is no different. Being shrewd and wise makes us well-rounded and capable enough to discern when to adjust our kindheartedness level. Yes, there are times when we must dial it up or turn it down a notch since we deal with individuals from diverse backgrounds. What works in one situation for one might not work for another.

SCENARIO

You, a guy, have a single-parent next-door neighbor with two small children who just lost her job (let's christen her Ms. Single Mom for clarity's sake). The job market has been rough post-pandemic, so you offer her a $100 food pantry gift certificate your job gives employees of the month. You didn't need it, so you paid it forward. The neighbor is somewhat sheepish but appreciative. Later that month, her car was repossessed because she couldn't keep up with payments. Feeling abundant empathy, you tune up an old beater hatchback collecting dust in your garage for the past two and a half years.

Days later, after you have completed the task, you ring her doorbell several times, and your neighbor opens the door. You deposit the keys in her hand, pointing at your freshly washed secondhand car. The smile fades from her face, and she aggressively hands you the keys back with a terse, "No, thank you; I'll be fine."

Dumbfounded, you walk home, wondering what you did wrong. You were kind, but it wasn't received. You're trying to shake it off a week later but still get upset when the incident crosses your mind. While out raking the yard, she comes outside and heads your way. Uh oh, you don't want any drama.

She confesses that times have indeed been hard for her since the breakup of her 10-year marriage and ex-husband leaving her for his perky 20-year-old massage therapist. Since then, she's been easy prey for predators, primarily men looking for their next meal. Trust is becoming more challenging because she's mistaken their ulterior motives for kindness. She accepted your first kind act because the refrigerator and cupboard were bare but felt the second one was a means for you to ask for something in return, namely her body.

Turning red, you tell her that it was the furthest thing from your mind and that you were genuinely offering help to someone in need as you hoped someone would do for you. Silence thickens the air as you both contemplate how you misread the situation. Finally, you gather yourself and let her know you're only steps away if she needs any no-strings-attached help. She shakes your hand with tears in her eyes, offering a heartfelt thank you.

People react how they've been acted upon!

Kindness

God made us with variable temperaments, which means we respond differently to adverse and favorable stimuli. In the above scenario, you recognize we don't react similarly to benevolence. The single mother had a hard turn in her life, leaving her wary of others' intentions. Looking outside, most would classify her as bitter and broken.

Not so fast, friends. I want to drive home the fact that we are multidimensional and complex because I feel we apply a "one size fits all" approach to life. Every human has gauged another's actions/reactions based on their own, which is normal. However, we must grow, understand, and value others' individuality. No two beings are alike, even with the same upbringing.

My journey isn't yours.

Ms. Single Mom let her past experiences shape her current outlook. It is naive to think you won't encounter a range of ideas/thoughts and never be tempted to speak/act out in cruelty or anger rather than kindness. She had every right to be angry at her ex-husband's betrayal and subsequent financial demise, but at what cost?

NOTE: There is nothing wrong with getting angry, but we shouldn't act out of anger. Not all anger is useless. Righteous anger is born from injustice to a person, group, place, or thing. I've become agitated, mad, and downright angry when I've learned of innocents being taken advantage of or persecuted. *Pure*, righteous anger or indignation (not what you see displayed on television and at rallies by crafty politicians angling for votes) is commonly defined as anger aroused by something unjust, unworthy, or mean (Merriam-Webster.com, 2024). Anger is healthy—until it's not.

DON'T SLEEP ON IT

Anger becomes a problem when you can't let it go, and it consumes your thoughts, decision-making skills, and movements. You can be righteously angry when you discover a coworker is stealing money from an orphanage fund, but you can't let it alter your character and foundational integrity. Anger, like any other emotion, must be processed. Recognize why you are upset, work through it, find a solution, then let it go—don't allow it to define you. Why? Anger has a way of taking over and spiraling out of control.

Ephesians 4:26 is a familiar verse. The New Living Translation reads, *"And don't sin by letting your anger control you. Don't let the sun go down while you are still angry."*

Notice it doesn't say you shouldn't get mad. God made us knowing our humanity would express a myriad of emotions. Our ability to monitor and control those unpredictable emotions separates us from other mammals and determines our likelihood of advancement.

If possible (I'm not referring to those issues that require long-term resolution), resolve the outrage before your head hits the pillow. Don't let it build and fester. Your mental well-being and that of your loved ones are protected when you empty your destructive thoughts before turning in at night. There's nothing worse than going to sleep with a heavy heart, whether it's filled with worry, doubt, or anger. I know I'm preaching to the choir. Try to sort out issues or at least create a plan of action to fix them as soon as possible.

Don't let those nagging thoughts stress you out and deprive you of much-needed sleep and energy. You can permit self-defeating views to bring fear, doubt, and anger or translate them into faith, assurance, and kindness. Why not rein in those distressing feelings and work them in your favor?

Can you harness those thoughts and ideas into something positive or kind, or do you veer towards negativity and unkindness? If you answer yes to the latter, remedial lessons are in order. Stop right here and do an honest-to-goodness self-assessment.

Our mind is our hard drive.
We must clean & clear
negative thoughts every
day so we operate at
maximum capacity.

Seriously, let's do it! Pause here and reason. Are you deliberately being kind to others, or do you use that time to be mean, snarky, and obnoxious? I'm asking about you, no one else. This is all about you. It's pointless to ponder who fits the above description without looking within first--you know, human tendency. Check out this scenario.

Scenario

Everyone in your social circle has been raving about a new psychology professor at your college. He offers a relaxed, highly interactive, and fun learning environment. It sounds like an easy A and a way to catch up on sleep. You sign up. By the second week, Professor Z discusses destructive narcissistic behaviors—your interest peaks. As the behaviors are read, you immediately start thinking of friends and family that fit the bill.

You mean business, even ripping out a sheet of paper (for quick disposal, of course—no need for those closest to you to know your true feelings and cause a stir) and begin listing and ranking them in order. Not once did you consider any of those behaviors match "your" character like a textbook description—word for word.

- ✓ Lacks compassion
- ✓ Avoids self-examination
- ✓ Arrogance is your by-name
- ✓ Shifts blame onto others
- ✓ Manipulation is your essential strategy

Those five traits should be checked off for you, not the ones you have in mind. The lack of self-awareness is astounding. You even considered recording the session and sending all the offenders an anonymous text via a burner phone. Wow!

How is it that we are so splendid at pointing out others' flaws and shortcomings but rarely take the time to reflect on the person we see staring back in the mirror? Michael Jackson was onto something with that 1988 chart-topping single, *Man in the Mirror*. One reflective verse declares we start with the person in the mirror and change their ways first.

We wouldn't have half the troubles plaguing society if we did this. Seriously, think before you speak. Look inside before looking out. I'll continue repeating that and other central exhortations until they stick. The change we seek in our communication, finances, health, profession, and relationships starts with us.

Likewise, kindness comes when you **want** to be kind and **decide** to do just that. Speaking kindly is in your grasp—reach for it and do it. No more "I'm trying". Isn't it amazing that somehow, we find the time, money, and energy to do what we want? Just do it. Talk is cheap. Anyone can say what they will do, but it takes determination and perseverance. We can't declare and decree that we want something different to occur in life and we are not willing to:

1. **Change our mindset**—a mindset is a set of attitudes. Attitudes are feelings and opinions. If your outlook is cynical, full of bitterness and unkindness, you'll have to replace it intentionally. Behavior, like mindset, isn't altered until something new and opposing is introduced. To change anything, a conscious decision is made to modify behavior. Make no mistake; change starts with change.

2. **Put in the work to make necessary changes** – It doesn't matter how badly you want it; if you're unwilling to do the legwork, you won't see a change. I can wish to be a bestselling author, but until I write

a book, it won't happen. I've got to put some legs (work) to my dreams for them to manifest and materialize. Millions of people have a vision, dream, or goal, but without a strategy or an executable plan, it will remain in their headspace until they die. Do you want to change? Get busy!

JUST BE KIND

No more facades, pretense, or fronting—just the real you. The one that is rarely seen. The true you behind those closed doors may not be as generous, forgiving, and <u>KIND</u>. I often say being open, honest, and transparent is a sign of maturity, but you must know *how* and to *what degree*.

Honesty and transparency are nothing without kindness attached. Kindness is an add-on, an extra feature honesty can't do without. They go hand in hand, like faith needs works. James 2:17 (NLT) says, *"In the same way, faith by itself if it is not accompanied by action, is dead."* Where you see one, you'll see the other, like salt and pepper.

When telling someone the cold, hard facts, it should be married with grace and mercy. Aggressive, in-your-face "this is the truth, take it or leave it" honesty is like trying to swallow a horse-sized vitamin. You know it's needed, but you wish it wasn't so hard to gulp down. Kindness is the water that helps the recipient receive and digest our words. Be open and forthright, but make sure kindness is interwoven.

 ## WHAT'S THE LESSON?

Being kind is a vital component of a mindset shift, and please know that any advancement is subject to relapse. You make a New Year's resolution to eat no more sweets, and a birthday party is held at your office the next day. What do you do? There are choices to make, for challenges **will** come.

Whether with a new diet or being kind, you'll be tempted to revert to the old you. Times will come when you want to give in to familiar feelings and let them rip and say not-so-nice things, but you'll think of this book and be reminded there are drawbacks to being unkind. Words have consequences, so you'll have to decide if you want to put out negativity and receive bushes and thorns or generate positivity and reap beautiful roses.

Kind words are useful carriers of life, and it doesn't cost us a thing to say them, except maybe our pride. It's time to throw pride out of your daily toolkit. You don't need it. It hinders and blocks you from progressing; no situation or person is worth losing out on your purpose. What does an aloof, standoffish attitude have to do with purpose, you ask? The day you decide to act ugly might be the day you receive a solution or answer to a problem.

Scenario 1

Your supervisor has been contemplating giving you, one of the company's loyal and most competent workers, a promotion.

But as you defiantly stomped to your desk, exchanging words with and flipping an equally combative coworker off, she changed her mind. Three long years, you've been agonizing over one, and you just ruined that chance in 15 seconds.

You can't expect to receive what you don't give.

Scenario 2

In the long department store checkout line, a stranger behind you sees you counting one-dollar bills and lining up pennies to pay for school clothing and tries to get your attention. You think he's upset you've taken almost two minutes to pay the cashier, and you say a couple of choice words to close his mouth for good. You didn't see the wad of cash in his hand extended towards you as a goodwill gesture.

YOU LOST OUT!

The money you hoped and prayed for was within reach, but unkindness got in the way. Instead of jumping into defense mode, be kind, and it'll find its way back. Ephesians 4:32a reminds us, *"Be ye kind one to another."* It's a two-way street; you can't expect to receive something you don't give. If you want kindness, sow it.

While we're on the topic of kindness, a little clarification is needed because it's regularly misunderstood. Kindness is often haphazardly lumped in with being simple-minded, weak, and lacking confidence. It's quite the opposite! A kind person isn't one that people walk all over or use and abuse. Individuals who are used and abused are those who "tend" to be fearful or have low esteem. It can undoubtedly be a mixture as well.

A person who loves to fight (not self-defense) might seem bold and courageous, but a lack of confidence is causing them to lash out at others and brawl—they are masking heartache with bravado. They're hurting because of something that transpired in *their* own life—it has little to do with the people they set their sights on.

Does this sound familiar? It's the short definition of a bully, a person who has been injured emotionally, physically, or sexually and doesn't know how to process the trauma they've sustained. We know "hurt people hurt others" and reject kindness because it leaves them vulnerable. Do you recognize a friend or loved one who struggles in this area? Or perhaps it could be you. The first step is admitting, right?

No one is left unscathed from the ravages of unkindness. Beneath our bright smiles, fancy clothing, and college degrees are wounds—some older than others. These are the ones we sustained in childhood, adolescence, and adulthood. We showed vulnerability and were rewarded with attacks from those who didn't know any better and those who did. Release them, don't hold them captive any longer.

When you think of the damaging occurrence, does it still sting, burn, or pulse? An unhealed wound still feels painful when you touch it and never seems to reach the "scar" stage. Either way, we must remove the poison (forgive) and let go (heal).

Lastly, a kind person knows who they are and is assured enough to defer to others when necessary; that's not weak. Just because you decide not to engage a liar, backstabber, or another with ill intentions doesn't mean you are feeble. It takes bravery and sophistication to say and do the right thing. Have I not hammered that point home?

As we grow up, we discern how to pick and choose which battles to fight so we can win the war. Resist urges to volley back, return fire, or clap back. Being kind doesn't cost you anything. I'm ready to be kind; what about you?

S – season

> "*A word spoken at the right time is like gold apples on a silver tray.*"
> **Proverbs 25:11 (HCSB)**

Yes, I added another letter to the acronym. The "S" stands for season. Even after you have thought about your words, they might still not be appropriate to speak at that time. After following the THINK model, you need to consider the right time. I know, I know...you thought I was finished. However, this is another step, another caution, if you will, that shouldn't be ignored. We must speak when it's fitting or simply the right time. Easier said than done?

The third chapter of Ecclesiastes is well known for its time rendering. I want to focus on the jewel verse 7b, "*a time to keep silence, and a time to speak.*" I don't have to continue in this chapter, for that verse said it all. **Not every thought that comes to your mind is meant to pass your lips.** That's an original Pamela quote—don't use it without giving me credit (just teasing).

A TIME TO BE QUIET, THEN SPEAK

Quiet Time

A time to be silent. Hmm, do we know when to hush? Honestly, I've missed the mark even after writing this book. It's a work in progress, not an overnight fix, but we improve with practice. As we evaluate our words and run them through the THINK filter, we must ask if the time is right. What you and I can impart might fit the model, but the timing is off, and it should wait until a more opportune time--perhaps a moment when we have a better understanding.

That's why we shouldn't be so quick to speak. James 1:19 (NIV) warns, *"My dear brothers and sisters, take notes of this: Everyone should be quick to listen, slow to speak, and slow to become angry."* No interpretation is needed. First and foremost, we should hear and listen before speaking. There is a difference.

Hearing is acknowledging sound. You're at home typing on your laptop, and the dishwasher is going, the washing machine is washing clothing, the neighbors are fighting, and your favorite show is playing on television. You vaguely hear background noises of the appliances in operation, the neighbors at each other's throats, and your favorite show. However, you are not listening to any of them. To listen is to devote your focus, energy, and time to an object, circumstance, or person(s). You hear the white noise of your surroundings, but you aren't focused on them. When we listen, we employ our senses to understand content and context.

Hearing comes before listening. Listening comes before speaking.

Let's dig a little deeper. Our world is/can be so fast-paced that we don't *pause* and *assess* before interjecting. Do you recall the scenario of the almost accomplice to bank robbers that could've been charged as an accessory to a crime? That's an extreme example. How about this one?

SCENARIO
A teacher at Nowhere High School is chatting it up with other teachers in the faculty lounge. She tells another that Ms. Smith was wearing a bad outfit today. Without proper contextual clues, the receiver (only hearing the content and not understanding cultural lingo, African American Vernacular English, shortened AAVE) may think the speaker was degrading Ms. Smith. The "bad" alluded to is a very agreeable or sharp outfit.

Teacher B leaves the breakroom and asks a staff member, a certified busybody, if they've seen said outfit. The busybody does what busybodies do: walks through the halls and spreads gossip that Ms. Smith is dressed like a floozy. The context was not correctly interpreted, and an extra layer of nasty was added.

Something so pure and innocent blows up into an argument, followed by hurt feelings and even the loss of a relationship. What was meant as a compliment is now the cause of tension and distrust among educators. To avoid confusion, the original speaker should have clarified what a "bad outfit" meant to a non-AAVE speaker.

This is a recurring theme. Countless people write others off because of a misconstrued sentence or phrase. This demonstrates how quickly we respond without having the complete picture. Be slow to speak because you might not have the whole story. I've had many blunders while stationed overseas where my polite smile or greeting was interpreted as a romantic interest. It's laughable now, but it was scary when the stranger reciprocated an interest I didn't have. Neither party had a full understanding of each other's social cues.

There are instances when we need to be quiet and listen. Being silent doesn't mean you have nothing to say or that you agree. It means you have assessed the matter and feel it's wise not to comment.

Speak on it

After assessing the situation, it may be time to speak up. Obviously, there are many more occasions when we should say something. One of life's great tragedies is when someone has a chance to speak up on another's behalf and doesn't. I'm not talking about standing up with deceitful ulterior motives--like saying something because it will garner you political, social, or monetary mileage—Basically, doing it for a show!

We should speak up as if we are the ones needing advocacy!

We've seen that. A person who only stands up when others are watching but would look the other way if there wasn't a spotlight shining on their "good deed." When I say speak on it, I mean doing the right thing to benefit the recipient. Hopefully, you are seeing or have seen the pattern. The T-H-I-N-K module is all about adding to, not taking away. Thinking before you speak allows you to concentrate on ways to support.

People tend to support those they see as worthy of support! We are more apt to speak up when we value others' humanity. That's why it's so essential to cultivate empathy and compassion across cultural, socioeconomic, and racial lines. Compassion says, "I place myself in your shoes and now understand your plight and what you're going through." 'I won't prejudge you based on my self-serving ideas or reasons."

The opposite of empathy is apathy, an "I don't care about you, only me" attitude. Unfortunately, more individuals fall into the latter category.

What's in it for me?

Modern society has steadily shifted towards a selfish, individualistic culture for several decades. An individualistic culture is driven by personal achievement, which is not terrible; however, group ideals and achievements are secondary, tertiary, or plain forgotten. Now add "extreme" to that definition. When it's all about you, it's truly all about you—with no concern for others. Concern for your fellow man and humanity is discarded or centered on an individual.

Fundamental individualism is a breeding ground for reward-based actions ➔ ➔ translation: if there's something in it for me, I will help you; if not, you're on your own. No wonder apathetic folk can walk by a woman being punched in the face and do nothing. I'm not saying to place yourself in a potentially fatal situation. Taking out your cell phone and dialing 911 is a start!

A combination of irreverent social mediums (ratings-obsessed television, alternate reality video gaming, popular social media websites), zealous peers, and misguided parents alike are teaching you to "stay out of it if it doesn't concern you" or "keep your mouth closed, it's none of your business." That may sound like solid advice for all states of affairs, but it's not.

What happens when your loved one needs help? Again, I'm not suggesting you put yourself in harm's way. I ask that you be willing to speak up or act in whatever capacity you can as if you were in that position and wanted someone to champion your cause.

If it's all about you, who else benefits?

Atrocious deeds have been committed and normalized worldwide because people have watched and said nothing because it "wasn't their problem" or "it doesn't affect me." Think about the cruel activities and remnants of enslavement toward Black Americans and other Indigenous populations across the globe. It was made possible for several reasons I won't go into for brevity, but a good history book (not one sanitized for the masses) will reveal.

It's time to responsibly speak up, not just when you have a dog in the fight! When you see an event unfolding, and it is unjust, don't just sit there. If you cannot say something, find someone else who can. Higher level living requires courage.

In fact, too many cowards are walking around masquerading as brave men and women, putting on a front until it's time to make a difference. It's like politicians promising the moon and stars but reneging as soon as pressure from corporations and rich donors mounts. All that talk about being the 'working man's man' goes out the window when money comes to the table—or should I say, 'under the table'?

People are only bona fide heroes (in my humble opinion) when they stand up in the face of adversity and persecution, not after. Had more courageous individuals stood up during history's most inhumane eras, millions wouldn't have suffered cruel and unwarranted treatment. A hero isn't like one sees in Hollywood action movies: imposing, muscled, brandishing a gun, or always male. A hero in the purest form is willing to stand up for what's right, not popular, in the face of opposition, expecting no reward or recognition. They've concluded a wrong must be righted and are often not hailed a hero until some time has passed.

A hero is willing to stand up for what is right, not what is easy and comfortable.

A perfect example is Dr. Martin Luther King Jr., who was perceived as an outside agitator by many in the South and treated accordingly. It wasn't until years after his assassination and a federal holiday named after him that his name evoked peace and righteousness. It's funny how the passage of time changes viewpoints.

I'm sure some didn't want to get involved in the Civil Rights era then or now. Don't get me wrong. Many avoid involvement out of fear of consequences: losing their job, facing threats, losing friendships or family connections—but I hope and pray you can sleep at night knowing you can right a wrong and won't. I take you back to an earlier question: what if it was you or a loved one in need? Would you still feel the same? Remember empathy! Empathy propels you into places where apathy says, "Don't go."

IN DUE SEASON

There was a famous song penned by Pete Seeger about seasons in the late 1950s that subsequently became a worldwide hit in 1965 titled "Turn! Turn! Turn!" It is arguably the most recognized non-Christian song that quotes scriptures from the Bible. The song uses the entire third chapter of Ecclesiastes and verse 1 as a chorus, which says, "To everything, there is a season and a time for every purpose under heaven." We've got to be in season; there's no way around it. Timing is critical. You can be in the right place at the wrong time—season matters! The two examples below highlight the gravity of timing.

Example 1

You finally have days off and spending money saved up for a break from your 9 to 5 job. The white sandy beaches and clean, crisp air call your name directly from the Caribbean.

This 7-day vacation will be heaven on earth, but you miscalculated the time to arrive at your nearest airport and are running late in traffic. As you race through gridlocked interstate exits and reach the terminal, you come only to find out your flight is taking off—what a bummer! You're at the right place, but your timing is off. The season to board that plane had a short window, and you missed it.

Example 2

You've been waiting for a major blockbuster to reach your local movie theater, and you can't wait to see it. Everything is fantastic—you left home on time (for once) and have your online receipt and some extra money for overpriced snacks and sugary watered-down soda pop (I couldn't resist that dig).

You're the first person at the ticket counter and wonder why no individuals are in line, and the cashier tells you the movie doesn't play until two hours later. Well, you're at the right place but at the wrong time. I don't care how much you want to see the movie—it's not happening. You'll be waiting a couple of hours until the doors open if you want to gaze at your favorite celebrity.

I said all that to tell you it's the same with our words. Are the words you speak in season? You might wonder what I mean by 'in season,' as though words could be out of season, like blooming roses in winter or fur-lined parkas in summer. There is a time, a suitable time to articulate words. I can think of many verbal exchanges where the information was true, helpful, inspirational, and kind—but it was not the right time.

Prepare the Word

Out-of-season words are spoken at the wrong time, and the receiver refuses to receive the information because **they** are not open. The words fell on fallow ground and didn't take root since the soil wasn't prepared to be cultivated. Nature plays this principle out right before our very eyes. A farmer can sow all they want, but if the ground is unyielding, the seed won't perform. I don't care how well-intentioned the farmer might be. The right or wrong time of the year makes all the difference.

You can pointlessly try to plow and dig up ground that isn't ready, whether frozen or dense and rock-laden. The land will refuse you because it hasn't warmed up or been prepared. That's why farmers are very particular about when they plant. They want the best yield for their work. We've got to be the same way when it comes to speaking.

Conversely, some can't accept a word because they don't have the capacity. Our ability to receive speaks to our level of maturation at that grade/level of our life. Just as a person can impart knowledge and wisdom to us during the right season, we might not be able to receive it because "**we're**" not ready.

Can You/They Handle It?

At some point in our lives, we've all been given information we weren't ready to handle because we were too emotionally or mentally immature. Chances are there was a little fear present, as immaturity and fear work and move as a team. I know that was a mouthful. Let's break it down.

What does it mean to be immature emotionally? Emotional health is *the ability to cope with positive and negative emotions in an appropriate way.* (WebMD Editorial Contributors, 2024). An emotionally healthy person knows how to express feelings in a way that doesn't intentionally harm him/herself or others. Likewise, an emotionally immature being doesn't have those processing skills.

Have you spoken to a person about their welfare (physical, financial, or otherwise), and you did everything right: you were truthful, helpful, inspirational, and kind, but you still couldn't reach them? The reason is they were not present! Present in the sense of being there (available physically and mentally).

Case in point, many parents are available in their child's life but not present. You can give your offspring clothing, gifts, and money, but raising a healthy, functioning young child who matures into a bright adult takes more than that. It takes love, care, discipline, time, and money. You should be present in your emotions as a parent is present in their child's life. I want to delve into emotional and mental immaturity a bit more, which is one of the main reasons we can't receive or give a word in due season.

Emotional Immaturity

When someone is emotionally immature, they struggle to accept words that could strengthen them. You'll also find it challenging to process correctly, which leads to:

1. Shutting down — when people shut down, they put up walls and barriers for protection. As previously mentioned, these same walls can imprison versus keep us safe. Not only will you erect walls, but you'll also check out. By checking out, you become emotionally unavailable, not there or anywhere else for that matter! You've experienced so much pain and decided it won't happen again, so you close that part of yourself off. We've all done it. Do *you* recall when you emotionally shut down? Those closest to you were trying to break that concrete barrier surrounding you, but it was stronger than your desire to be free. My friend, don't shut down because you keep out the solutions.

2. Lashing out happens when anger and frustration build up, and you take that dissatisfaction out on another. Take a devoted but frustrated husband. He comes home from work fed up with low pay and disrespect from his superiors but chooses to belittle his wife and children instead of dealing with low self-esteem derived from his perceived lack of provision. He wants to tell the shift manager what he thinks of him and his job but is wise enough not to. The lack of resolution results in him and us taking it out on those we love and want the best for us rather than those who are inflicting anguish. Your action is a result of how YOU feel. Instead of lashing out, concentrate

on healing within and finding creative outlets to deal with unfulfillment.

Mental Immaturity

We've covered how emotional immaturity ties into our inability to receive. Now, let's move on to mental instability. According to the World Health Organization, mental health is *a state of well-being in which every individual realizes his or her potential, copes with everyday life stresses, works productively, and contributes to their community.* (Mental Health: Strenghtening Our Response, 2022). That's an incredibly long definition. I loosely define it as a person's mindset, a set of attitudes.

What does it mean to be mentally immature and absent? A mentally absent and immature individual has a perception block. They can't see past their own set of established attitudes. It's like traveling down a two-way road with a roadblock. You must wait until that block is removed, or you will become stuck in the same position for who knows how long. When you have a blockage:

1. **You can't receive anything new** – the mental block makes it difficult to accept new information. Have you ever tried to fill your car's oil reservoir, but something blocked the flow? No matter how much you poured, the container refused the liquid, which eventually had to be unstopped. We are like that oil tank, unable to be poured into because we lack mental

maturity. You're stuck in preconceived notions and not present mentally. There's an idiom: the older you get, the more set you become in your ways. Are you old and set? Does meeting people from different backgrounds scare you? If so, you might have a block. Also, anything innovative is seen as a challenge and threat to the normalcy of the mentally immature. This applies to life in general. I'm sure you are already thinking of some areas in your own life where you need to shore it up.

2. **You must make a choice to remove the impediment or stay stagnant** – moving out of a fixed place requires an intentional and conscious effort. It's as if you're stopped at a red light at a busy intersection, and the light has turned green. The light changing colors means absolutely nothing if you're unwilling to move. You must take your foot off the brake and press the gas pedal to advance the car. You can wish, hope, and even pray that the vehicle will move from an idle position to one of movement. It won't. If you are parked mentally, you must actively engage your foot (mind) and get rolling again. You have the power, my friend. Will you allow a closed-off mindset to hinder you from receiving a word in season? Don't miss out on what life offers because YOU are trapped. Shake off your grave clothes and live. You've been dead long enough!

 **WHAT'S THE LESSON?**

This chapter was filled with insights on giving and receiving communication because "getting there" requires attuning to your surroundings and being. Your body signals you to eat, sleep, and use the restroom. Similarly, we need to sense when it's time to receive and give a word in due season. God will send people into your life to assist you on your journey as He's using you in another's. Don't dismiss someone because they don't look, speak, or act like you. That disheveled person you're trying to avoid could be the answer to your problem or a catalyst for a breakthrough. Remember, His ways are not our ways.

A closed mind is a stagnant mind.

"Wisdom is the principal thing; therefore, get wisdom; and with all thy getting get understanding." That jewel is Proverbs 4:7. Wisdom is what we should go after, not connections or shortcut hook-ups. Those things will come when you employ insight. While you're at it, pursue understanding, not a beautiful/handsome face with a killer body or material possessions that deteriorate and decline in value. No, I want

you to have something that improves with time: wisdom and understanding.

In sharing the T-H-I-N-K principle, I want you to walk away with a solid understanding of effective communication and integral living. If we want to manifest our purpose, knowing what it is and how to use it is essential—that's what understanding does for you. Understand when it's appropriate to speak versus talk. I equate talking to an automatic reflex or action like blinking. Even without thinking, you blink your eyes, yawn, burp, or sneeze. A stranger says hello, and you say hello in return (or not, depending on the region and customs of the country).

However, speaking in its natural form requires thought. Think about it: you've never heard someone say they're preparing for a 'talking' engagement. They are attending a speaking engagement. Public speakers, motivators, and life coaches invest countless hours perfecting their craft. They intentionally study and rehearse what they present to an organization, crowd, or small group. Even off-the-cuff extemporaneous speakers practice in their heads.

Henceforth, when we speak, it will be calculated to affect the change we intend—no more flying by the seat of our pants, skinny jeans, short shorts, or warm-ups. We take authority and exert power over our thoughts, tongue, and content projected in the environment. Know WHO and WHERE you are in life, and let your words reflect that knowledge. Build your courage and character to be the great person you're destined to be.

We're speaking nothing but awesomeness from now on. That potential inside you has been locked away for years; now it's time to let it loose. You can *speak* it into existence as you *talk* yourself into a mess. Speaking the right thing at the wrong time can be just as detrimental as saying something inappropriate or nothing at all.

This concludes part 1 of our exploration of thinking for next-level living. Let's move on to why we should. Go on and grab another cup of your favorite beverage, for there's more to discover.

PART 2
You Should...

Why?

"Death and life are in the power of the tongue, and those who love it will eat its fruit."
Proverbs 18:21 (NASB)

Maybe there's still a nagging "why" you are contemplating/and or struggling with. You don't see the big deal and wonder why "I should be *concerned* about the words leaving my mouth." Why ***do*** we need to watch what we say?

Three words: Words have power! If you don't believe words have power, think back to when a word or words transformed your life for the better or worse. I distinctly remember the first time I was called the N-word. I was in the fourth grade and on the playground, one of my favorite places besides the library. The physical education teacher was leading us in a new game and told all students to hold hands with one another for an exercise. A mousy brown-haired girl declared that she didn't want to hold hands with a n_____. Another black girl roughly yanked her hand and held it instead of me.

Those words had an impact. They revealed her character, and I decided she was someone I didn't want to be around. This occurred in the 1970s, but unfortunately, the more things change, the more they stay the same. Racial epithets and xenophobic chants are still strewn about globally, not just in the United States in conservative enclaves.

Sticks and stones may break my bones and words can surely hurt me!

Reflect for a minute: a parent, trusted mentor, or another person in authority spoke great things about you, and those words caused you to feel fantastic—they boosted your self-esteem and self-worth a million times over. Or the opposite happened, and you were called stupid, ugly, fat, or worthless. Those words cut deep, and you've been carrying them ever since.

You put on a brave face in front of loved ones, friends, and co-workers, but you are emotionally and mentally damaged on the inside. Only you know the pain, embarrassment, and shame you hide. You try to block it/them (the words) out, but they are like an old vinyl record on repeat, slowly wearing itself out.

Those familiar with long-playing (LP) records know the plastic material can be scratched, but it will still play. The sound and beat may be slightly warped, and it might skip, but you can make out the words. Can you still hear the hurtful words spoken to you years ago?

Our thoughts control our tongue. Let's give credit where credit is due!

LIVE OR DIE

Words must be wisely spoken. Proverbs chapter 18 verse 21, yet another oft-quoted scripture, reminds us life and death are in the power of the tongue, and those who love it will eat its fruit. You and I do wield power. I've said it so many times. I feel like that LP. I don't care if you are from a developing country living in abject poverty; you still have power—the power of speech. That remains the one thing you can control and is within your area of responsibility. That child on the playground had the option to refrain from spreading her brand of hateful ideology or voicing it so all in earshot would know her racist thoughts.

Our words either give life or bring death. Thank God, her words didn't break me. Even at that age, something inside (besides my parents' teaching) told me I was more than enough, and I acted accordingly. I urge parents to build up their child's self-esteem before entering public or private school. You are their first teacher! Carve out a minute or two for daily affirmations and self-esteem lessons utilizing whatever tools work best. I had mine.

However, most of us are not fortunate enough to sidestep the arrows of callousness, thereby sustaining deep wounds when offensive words are spewed. Again, power resides in our speech. You don't need to physically harm someone to destroy them—words can do the job just as easily, whether spoken to their face or behind their back. A person's character can be killed with false accusations; the legal term is defamation.

Defamation occurs when you make these claims to a third party. The legal system takes this seriously. Why can't we? The glib words we speak knowingly or unknowingly cause upset. Is that what we intend when we talk to our fellow man? I know the aim/goal of some hardened-hearted folk is to do exactly that. However, I don't think the average (read non-narcissistic, psychopathic) human being's intentions are in their heart to wound.

OUR tongue, which is controlled by our thoughts, brings forth life or pronounces death. If we choose to use life-giving words, we will reap life, and the opposite holds true as well. This is one critical reason we should think about our words. Virtuous words are like medicine, but bad words are like vomiting; once they start flowing, they can't stop. You can't retrieve vomit or bad words.

NO DO OVERS!

Once words are released into the atmosphere, they can't be taken back. Life is not a piece of lined writing paper with a jumbo No. 2 pencil dancing on the page, ready for you to erase any/all mistakes. No, you don't get a do-over. We can't say, "Oops, that didn't come out right…let me pull that back in." Remember, it's one of those "open mouth, insert foot" moments where taking the foot out does nothing but empty your cavity for more foolishness to spew forth or a contrite request for forgiveness. You might have the opportunity to apologize and make amends. What you can't do is turn back time; that's fiction.

There was an action television show on the CBS and Warner Brothers (CW) network called "*The Flash*," which ran for nine seasons (Oct 2014 – May 2023). I watched it faithfully every Tuesday. In the comic book and show, the protagonist, Barry Allen, can travel back in time due to a workplace accident in which he is struck by lightning and given superhero abilities.

Visualize the impact of your words before vocalizing them!

He has been favored with supersonic speed, which allows him to travel and fix future and past events. Of course, this enormous responsibility has consequences, and he mucks up quite a few things, including the lives of loved ones, strangers, and himself, in the quest to "right wrongs."

It would be nice to be Barry and return to *fix* things—we can't. Therefore, we must get it right the first time as often as possible. Words fly out of our mouths and speed toward someone or a group. They are just like bullets fired from a gun. There is no recall mechanism for firearms.

I understood this principle most when I had to qualify for the M-9 or M-16 in the Air Force. When my finger gripped the handle, I aimed to hit something. After pulling the trigger, that piece of dislodged metal was headed for its target—the target the sender intended. I could not stop the weapon's action—there was no turning back.

You can't take words back, either. As soon as we open our mouths (pull the trigger), the words fly out (bullet) and will either miss the target or hit a bull's eye, depending on our accuracy. Often, we fire a shot right in the chest or head of an individual, not even caring. That's how powerful words are!

I use this analogy because much of our conversation, especially in Western society, is so spontaneous that we rarely consider the possible fallout. Carelessly spoken words injure. Likewise, "the right word at the right time is like a custom-made piece of jewelry" Proverbs 25:11 (MSG). Translation: personalized jewelry is a magnificent thing of beauty and possesses excellent workmanship—so are the words spoken at the right time.

Our words frame and produce our destiny; our thoughts are the building blocks. God Himself thought about creating the world and spoke it into existence. Consequently, thinking is rudimentary to all endeavors we undertake in life. What we dwell on is usually what we'll produce.

Negative thinking creates negative actions, which produce negative results—there is no way around it. Instead of dwelling on self-defeating thoughts about how you or someone else isn't good enough, think positively about who you are and walk in purpose. Negativity flows into all areas and, more importantly, our relationships.

Relationships Lost

How do our words affect relationships? I'm referring to business and personal (friends, relatives, and marital). *Psychology Today* proclaims issues with communication are the number five reason why couples divorce (Ni, 2015). Sound familiar? One spouse calls the other stupid, and the offended retaliates with a swear word—no communication, just ill-prepared words and heated talk. Business deals and partnerships often fall apart because of poor or inadequate communication. We've got to learn and practice better conveyance skills. Check out the two scenarios below to see how quickly a connection sours.

Words spoken at the right time restore heavy hearts.

Scenario 1

Partner A bought a new copier machine without informing Partner B. Now; their business has a returned check that bounced back to them for insufficient funds. Partner A didn't check with B; had he checked, he would have known their last significant acquisition placed them in the red, and any new purchases would have to wait until the next fiscal year. Distrust, anger, and a possible business dissolution ensue.

A simple text or phone call inquiring about the co-owned company's latest financial status could've prevented the fiasco. Communication is a two-way street.

Scenario 2

Two friends talk weekly on the phone and have known each other for almost 20 years. One of their parents died, and the other knows it but doesn't call to give condolences or check on the friend's mental and emotional state. The grieving friend now doesn't trust the other friend and is standoffish when that person does call three months later asking if they want to go on a pleasure trip as if nothing happened. A once close twenty-year friendship has been jeopardized because of the communication gap.

What should've happened? The bereaved might have expressed his/her feelings at the perceived lack of care displayed by the friend. Perhaps the friend doesn't have the best social skills or can't handle death well.

These scenarios show how easily relationships can break down due to a lack of communication. Some associations can be salvaged after suffering damage, but others are lost forever. I'd hate to see anyone lose out on a precious bond due to words said or not said. Tried and true relationships are worth fighting for, but if one party is determined not to make it work, you must move on. This not only benefits you but them as well. They're not able to appreciate you in this season or ever. The loss is theirs, but you'll feel all the better knowing you put in an effort to right the wrongs. Not only do the right words salvage relationships, but they can charter your route to your goals.

Don't assume--talk it out!

THE RIGHT WORDS CAN FORGE A PATH TO PURPOSE AND DESTINY

How can your words chart your path? Being known for competent, fair, and courteous speech attracts the right people in your life. I'm not here to promote any 'new thought' philosophy of "putting things in the universe that you want to come back to you." Please hear me; I'm not criticizing or trying to delegitimize that concept. Millions of people ascribe to it—I don't.

I understand that some may strongly disagree with my Christian beliefs and teachings. To that, I say, "It's a free world." Adults can agree to disagree about politics, religion, or the origin of mankind. As long as you are respectful while presenting your side, there's no problem. Now that we've cleared that up let's move forward.

My spiritual point of reference for words making way for you is Ecclesiastes 10:12a, *"The words of a wise man's mouth are gracious and win him favor, but the lips of a fool consume him."* Favor comes chasing after you when you are wise in speech and deed. A level of trust is afforded you when knowledge comes from your mouth. Don't you like fellowshipping with people who "know" something and aren't afraid to share? You sit there and bask in their words seasoned with time, experience, and grace. You're more likely to assist them than the one spouting foolishly.

A fool's mouth brings him and you trouble if you heed his words...

Maybe you're a business entrepreneur, teacher, pastor, or lawyer and desire favor. Continue to be a person of excellence, and those doors will open. The opportunities you've been waiting on will present themselves. Trustworthy and dependable people will begin to find you. Birds of a feather will always flock together. Believe me; a helper bird is headed your way—they are attracted to your ethics and integrity. Need I remind you our reputation precedes us? Will it gain us access or have the door slammed shut in our faces?

IT COMES BACK TO YOU!

We are now at the last point, if not the most critical part of WHY we should think before we speak. What you say or do will come back to you. What you send out in words or deeds will eventually come back home to the owner, just like an expertly thrown boomerang. Those negative, taunting, demeaning words will visit when least expected.

You may have turned around and made a 180-degree turn from the old you. However, there is a spiritual truth we can't ignore: you reap what you sow. I know some of you were waiting for me to say it. Whatever expression you prefer—'what goes around comes around,' 'what you give is what you get'—the idea remains the same. A Biblical scriptural text has us covered.

Galatians 6:7b, *"Whatsoever a man soweth, that shall he also reap."* We can try another if the King James Version sounds slightly dated and stiff. The New Living translation reads, *"You will always harvest what you plant."* The seeds you and I plant will eventually sprout and bear fruit. As mentioned earlier, I'm an avid gardener and can testify that a harvest is coming our way regardless of how we've sown it. I've unintentionally dropped seeds on the way to my raised garden beds, only to see plants sprouting months later, and I wondered how they got there.

Those flippant words spoken in sarcastic jest are not exempt. We all have to work on it. You may not have meant any harm and just spouted off the first thing that came to mind, but the words have been given a mission to perform, and they'll do just that.

Those who intentionally sow damaging seeds are devious people who spread deceit, and they will reap that and other unpleasantness. Do you deliberately speak untruthfully, are unhelpful, try your best to be uninspiring, talk when it's not needed, and say unkind things? Well, my dear friend, that's what headed your way. The most soothing or dreadful (depending on your character and actions) aspect of reaping and sowing is you always get more back than what you put in.

Practical application:
Let's get practical, especially in areas like finances. Those of us building up wealth for a generational legacy understand that placing your money in a financial medium (usually) yields considerably more than what you initially put into the account. This is a significant feature we miss in the reaping and sowing principle. You know it, a scenario is next.

Scenario

You decide that a little fabrication on your income tax is harmless. The conversation in your head might go like this: 'The crooked government takes so much out of my hard-earned paycheck anyway, so I'm just taking what's rightfully mine. Hmm! They're not going to miss a couple of dollars."

The next thing you know, you receive an audit letter from the IRS for possible fraud and fail the subsequent review. Your choices are salary garnishment or a lump sum payment made out to one of the most hated institutions. At least that's what I've heard. If you'd done your research, you'd know that cheating on your taxes—even for a small amount like $1,000—can lead to fines of up to $250,000 and up to 3 years in prison. How's that for a return?

That reaping and sowing is something else, isn't it? The example of the farmer shows what we can expect if we do the right thing. A farmer plants a seed in the hope that he or she will harvest ten times, if not more, than what was initially sown. It's an investment principle (spiritual and natural). Now, think of your words in this light.

Each time you open your mouth, you invest in a bountiful harvest of blessings or curses. Again, our tongue is the rudder that will steer us on a path and journey to success or destruction. That small organ can shipwreck or bring us to a safe harbor. If this doesn't make you pause and think before you speak, I don't know what will!

No Time Limit

Whether your past actions were virtuous or dishonest, they will come back to you in due time. Reaping and sowing have no statute of limitations.

A statute of limitations is a law that expressly prohibits a lawyer from prosecuting a crime committed after a specified time limit. By law, you can get away with a crime if the set time has passed. If you've watched dozens of true crime documentaries, you've seen an episode where a sleazy criminal slithered his way out of punishment because cops bumbled evidence, the lawyers were inept, or the would-be felon was crafty enough to evade capture.

> Be steadfast, the good you did in the past will be rewarded in the future!

The sinking feeling of knowing justice wouldn't be handed out appropriately turned your stomach. Spiritual justice, however, works differently. All the right things (seeds) you've set in motion are not in vain. Verse 9 of the same chapter, Galatians 6, reminds us we will reap if we faint not. I know it can be challenging, but life itself is problematic. Some days, it will rain, but soon enough, the sun will shine again. Keep on believing.

Faith is the key! Living a remarkable spiritual life means walking in faith. Faith is seeing your life through the eyes of God. It doesn't matter if you can't see it or feel it. God already sees you living abundantly and purposefully in every area of your life. Stay focused on the path God has charted for your life. Don't allow circumstances and experiences to make you bitter and despondent. It won't always be this way.

Observe nature and let it teach you a thing or two. Nature shows us that fruit often appears and blooms after storms and rain. It might not look good now, but keep the faith, for the bounty you reap, might come in a day, week, month, year, or decade. No one knows when; we know it happens.

And it Happened!

Do you remember the story I relayed back in the **HELPFUL** chapter? The one where I was sent the long way to my second overseas duty location? The married vindictive guy who sought to teach me a lesson? Well, I'm not done with that story—it's the perfect example of reaping what you've sown through your words and deeds.

Before leaving that base, I found a dropped wallet outside our secure facility. It was slightly debris-covered, so I knew it hadn't been there long. I retrieved the wallet, found the military identification card, and looked up the owner (a guy) on a database locator. Upon learning his billfold, filled to the brim with money, had been found and secured, he profusely thanked me because he was panicking. He didn't know where he had left it and was overjoyed that someone was honest enough to return it.

The guy was ecstatic and offered me a reward, but I declined. That's what we are supposed to do—be true, helpful, inspiring, and kind. I was happy to do something for someone because I'd want the same courtesy extended. I wasn't expecting a reward. We should do things out of the kindness of our hearts, not selfish gain. When you have that attitude, you won't be upset if your kind act isn't broadcasted or recognized. Even if he hadn't offered compensation, I would've been fine. God repays those who do the right thing!

Back to the story. Fast forward about ten months later, after finding and returning the wallet, I'm stranded in a military terminal. Thanks to the revengeful sergeant from my last base,

I'm in a foreign country without transportation or money. This was about 1991, so personal cell phones were not an option, and ATMs were not readily available on military bases. Saying I was sweating bullets is an understatement. I started to get nervous because the next flight to my actual destination wouldn't leave until a couple of days later. I didn't know anyone there to call for help; the sergeants behind the desk wanted me out of the way, and I was cashless. What a mess!

Good deeds are like boomerangs; they eventually return to you.

I stood by the door, unsure what to do. I must have looked distraught because a uniformed person approached me and asked if anything was the matter, and I told him my plight. He offered to take me to the local finance office to get an advance on travel pay and to drive me off base since the billeting arrangements had to be made weeks in advance, and they had no vacancies anyway.

He was a perfect gentleman, no funny stuff—no lewd talk or behavior. I was helped to settle in for the time I was there. He took a personal day off and gave me a tour of the base and local sites, visited shopping markets, and drove me back to the terminal on my day of departure.

And guess what, my friend? It was the same guy whose wallet I found and returned at my first duty station almost a year earlier. Imagine my surprise and delight to see a familiar face. I'd only been in the Air Force for two years—a newbie, so I didn't know any other airmen outside of my previous base. You can call it coincidence or fate. I call it divine intervention via the reaping and sowing principle.

What are the odds of me meeting the same person I'd helped earlier? He was in the exact location at the right time when I needed help. Come on now—the odds of that happening are probably a million to one. When we say and do the right thing, we better expect payment in kind.

That may sound corny and be grammatically incorrect, but it's true. Do what's right, and right will have no choice but to show up on your behalf at just the right time. So, don't be weary in well doing. We WILL reap if we faint not! There's no limit on when your blessing(s) will appear.

 WHAT'S THE LESSON?

I know you'll agree when I say this chapter tells its own lesson. Integrity is critical, even when it hurts. Don't shy away from speaking what is TRUE, HELPFUL, INSPIRING, NECESSARY, and KIND. Don't forget it should be in SEASON too! You never know when your good stewardship will be rewarded.

PART 3
Barriers…

Barriers

"Barriers are what we erect after experiencing pain, trauma, and loss. Breakthroughs are what we experience after realizing those hurdles can be moved—by us!"
Pamela D. Foster

I contemplated whether to include this brief chapter because it felt like a rehash. But I started thinking (yes, I finally got the chance to use that pun) and realized you can follow the model and still come up short. You have all the ingredients, but some are missing or in low quantities. Revisiting the cake analogy, all the baking materials can be present, but the result is bland if you don't have enough of one or two. The right ingredients are important, and so is our maturity level.

As children, our parents told us we were not old enough to eat certain foods. I remember special occasions when we children ate hamburgers and hot dogs while the older crowd had heartier meals. We were told we were not big enough, meaning our palates hadn't developed to the point we'd appreciate what we were taking in. We were not seasoned enough to process the cuisine.

MATURITY.
Emotional and mental immaturity were discussed in the S-Season section and will reappear here as our unchecked emotions tend to be our most significant barriers. Let's find out how to get rid of them.

OBSTACLES, MOVE OUT THE WAY

Emotional Damage
In this year of our Lord 2024, I have noticed the average person is emotionally unstable. We've become desensitized to violence and overly sensitive to common sense. You never know what will set them off. It could be a glance or word. I'm not suggesting past generations had it all together because they didn't. There is truly nothing new under the sun. What we see now, in some facet, has already transpired in another decade or century. However, societal norms then dictated that you rein in your issues for the greater good. You were expected to endure and be more durable. Head held high, chin up now.

Growing up, neighborhood children would climb trees, fall, and injure themselves. They only went to the hospital if they were rendered unconscious or a bone was sticking out. I remember one day, I was out playing on a makeshift black rubber rope swing looped over a low tree branch. It was flexible and could be twisted for a fast, unwinding experience. I did that, not realizing an old tire iron wheel was near the tree root. As I made my last turn, my left knee struck the wheel and was cut deeply.

Looking down at the blood and the open wound, I was in shock. My first thought was to find a Band-Aid. I didn't tell my parents. Transpose that to today. An ambulance would be called, and somehow law enforcement would get wind of it, who more than likely would phone child protective services warning them of a negligent mother not properly caring for her six-year-old child.

What we could "stand" or "take" on yesteryear is not the same today, nor should it be. The point is that emotional maturation, or a lack thereof, flows into our speech. Anger, envy, fear, and guilt are just four emotions that cause one to speak inappropriately, accompanied by some personal examples.

1. **Anger** – Speaking while angry has to be the most dangerous time to articulate your thoughts. Fights have started, jobs have been terminated, political enemies have been made, friendships have dissolved, and lives have been lost. What do you do when feeling fury bubbling to the surface?

    a. STOP—Stop and breathe in and out before you start cussing or throwing hands. This slows your fight-or-flight response and allows you to assess the circumstances before they escalate to the point of no return.

b. Decide your desired outcome - Do you want to tell a cop about to arrest you for speeding that he's a modern-day Barney Fife? If you don't mind having a record and facing unemployment, go for it.

c. Weigh the impact – Answer how the outcome will affect you and your family. Are you okay that you will embarrass/shame your loved ones with a mugshot broadcast over the news and social media?

2. **Fear** – Fear is a gateway emotion that can be hard to detect. When a person is fearful, they may feel anger, impulsiveness, revenge, etc. These and many other emotions are fear masquerading. We fear and then act it out in many ways. It's insidious that we lose our voice when not speaking up/out. It causes us not to speak or speak to our detriment. Imagine your neighbor is a porch pirate (steals packages), and you're afraid to say something because you want to remain neutral and avoid clashes. You become their next unwitting victim months later after getting a ping from FEDEX that your $500 Nordstrom black cocktail dress has arrived. It wasn't at your door when

you got home. The pirate struck again, and now you want to get the homeowners association involved. Fear won. How do you combat it?

    a. Acknowledge your fear – Name what is making you afraid.

    b. Pinpoint the source – Do you remember the moment, or has it been so long that it seems it was always there? Reflect on when, where, how, and who. Once you've established "it," you can strategize.

    c. Formulate/engage a plan of attack – What will your plan include?

        i. Know your triggers – what/who seems to cause a flare-up?

        ii. Workarounds – How do you work around it until it's conquered? You can try positive guided imagery, therapy, homeopathic remedies, breathing exercises, or spiritual counseling. This list is endless.

3. **Jealousy** – Jealousy is envy's meaner and more threatening twin. Whereas envy encompasses admiration and displeasure, jealousy needs to humble its object

of resentment. Take two brothers who've been competitive since childhood and have allowed it to grow dark. One of their businesses just won a million-dollar contract, and the other's is barely scraping by. With the failing company, Brother B feels he should've gotten it and starts a rumor that Brother A bribed the contractor and did some illegal transactions. The contract has been withdrawn and put on hold, and there's an open investigation. Brother A's reputation has been questioned, and he is losing hard-earned clients. Because of an unchecked emotion, a business and family relationship is in jeopardy. What could Brother B have done differently?

a. Understood genuine emotions – We can mask our authentic feelings about one another until the real one emerges. Competition was a mere cloak for the seething jealousy lurking beneath. "Be true to you" first.

b. Push pause – Humans have a built-in stopgap. This temporary measure is used in emergencies until a more permanent one can be obtained. As the negative emotion boils to the surface, we can stop it from translating into harmful words.

c. Table It – It might be best to exit the conversation or engagement and walk away. That's it. If necessary, reconvene after acknowledging and doing the work to identify, heal, and recover from jealous intentions.

4. **Guilt** – Guilt appears when we regret a decision, an action, or an inaction. Remorse is complex because you might not have a clear solution. Speaking out of guilt places you at a disadvantage because you wish to right an actual or perceived wrong. In doing that, you can overcorrect or overcompensate. **TRIGGER WARNING:** The scenario contains sexual abuse. What if you, a parent, have a 10-year-old boy who is molested by his youth pastor at church? Your feelings are all over the place, from actual murder to burning down the sanctuary. After much assistance, you've calmed down. You promise your son the world and that you will always be there and never let anything bad happen to him again. As a result, your child uses expensive gifts as a coping mechanism and a way to feel in control of his life again, and you oblige with a dwindling bank account. What could you have done differently?

   a. Gather Your Thoughts—Traumatic events require patience, empathy, and wisdom. Prudence involves not acting rashly and not making promises you won't keep. Comfort the victim of abuse first, then act.

b. Seek wise counsel – Secure counsel in the form of approved and accredited personnel with a specialty in your need of care. Trauma can change your brain chemistry and should be treated by professionals only (University of Rochester Medical Center, 2022). Offering support and a listening ear is fine, but please leave the other stuff to the pros.

Impairments

Years ago, I read an online article about celebrities and their undisclosed imperfections. The list included those with six digits (fingers and toes), deformed appendages, heterochromia (eyes of different colors), extra nipples, webbed feet, and so on. The writer suggested that what we see on screen is manufactured by Hollywood: straight, pearly white teeth, flawless skin, low to no body fat, taut, tanned bodies, and perfectly coiffed hairstyles. In summary, no one is perfect. Everyone has flaws, both seen and unseen. Let's discuss three.

1. **Speech Disorders**—Impediments can present as early as a child learning to talk or occur later in life via a medical mishap, accident, or neurological deficit. Stuttering, lisping, and Tourette's are among those most widely known, and they significantly affect a speaker's confidence and ability to participate fully in society. What can you do to work around it?

a. Operate on Your Level—If your disorder worsens around crowds, adjust your circle to a more manageable group. Don't allow others to push you above your speech proficiency.

b. Limit Use or Find Alternative Means—Maybe your spoken language ability has diminished or is barely intelligible. Augmentative and alternative communication devices are available to assist people with communication disorders. If the idea of artificial assistance feels off, you can use electronic means (text, e-mail). The most important thing is to make your voice heard, literally. You have a right to a voice.

2. **Education Level** – This is a touchy one. One train of thought is that only academia or those with an advanced degree are credible and should expound upon specific topics. If you are not credentialed to their satisfaction, you will likely experience education bias. About 75% of my military career was spent working on a base/wing commander's administrative staff. The officer's quarterly and yearly awards reached my desk for quality control before going to the executive assistant and vice commander. There was always a rack and stack of who was more "deserving." It didn't escape me that those with the highest education were

top picks. What should you do if you've never cared to pursue higher education?

a. Understand Your Worth – An education is helpful, but career progression doesn't end there. There are countless stories of celebrities and businesspeople who never obtained a bachelor's, master's, or doctorate and managed to be successful. Their voices have been amplified because of their ability, not an expensive piece of paper.

b. It's What You Make It—Education is not always learned in a classroom. You may be book-smart but have no common sense. No one has a right to minimize the knowledge and contributions gathered outside a school. Frankly, our country is built upon entrepreneurial rags-to-riches stories, which are American bedrocks.

3. **Handicaps** – The word has evolved over the years. Decades ago, it was seen as a deficiency and almost something to be pitied. Of course, programs like the Special Olympics, founded in 1968, existed, but a certain dignity and laws against bias were lacking. It was not until the American Disabilities Act of 1990 that discrimination against a disabled person was prohibited. Even still, the stigma of having a "defective" body

or mind is being fought today. How do you keep your voice?

a. Stand Tall—Whatever your disability, you are whole. You may be missing extremities, paralyzed, or have a congenital disease, but you are not lacking. What you say is just as important as the next person. If someone tries to ignore you, let your presence be known. Not rudely, but assertively. "I'm here, and I have something to say."

b. Report If You Must – Often, a stronger person will try to assert authority over the weaker—essentially, a bully. Unfortunately, as we've read about and seen, the human condition influences some to punch down. Punching down is verbally attacking or criticizing someone you perceive as in a worse or less powerful position than you (Cambridge University Press & Assessment, 2024). If you're at your job and think you may be a victim due to your disability, report him/her or them. File a complaint with your Equal Employment Opportunity Commission.

WHAT'S THE LESSON?

Barriers will always present themselves. It's a part of living we can't escape. Socioeconomic status, gender, national origin, or skin color won't prevent you from encountering hurdles. The more we advance, the more they come. However, some can be removed. Some you'll have to jump over. Some you can go around. You'll have to go through others. Speaking barriers are no different.

Anger, fear, jealousy, and guilt are emotional barriers. Emotions can be trained and managed. For example, a preschool child's parents teach him to control outbursts because they know he will be a detriment to his teacher, classmates, and himself. We will adjust once we've concluded that there will be consequences for our emotional volatility.

What we see as our deficiencies can work for us if we're willing to understand and build on our limitations. Franklin D. Roosevelt, a shrewd politician, contracted polio in 1921 at age 39. His closest advisors championed his political aspirations when he appeared at a convention in 1924 while assisted with braces and crutches. Nine years later, he became the 32nd president of the United States. NEVER GIVE UP.

CONCLUSION

Okay, my friend (I think I can call you that now, right?), we've come to the end of this discussion on speaking before you T-H-I-N-K. We've laughed, shared a journey of words and stories, contemplated our thoughts about life, and are now ready to implement what we know.

I hope you've either gained new insights or refreshed your memory and have been reminded that comprehensive thinking is essential for productive communication. Comprehensive thinking means it's complete, detailed, and wide-ranging. Productive communication is thoroughly evaluated beforehand.

Much like going before your workplace supervisors in a staff meeting, you're crossing every "t" and dotting every "i" in advance because your reputation (and job) is on the line. Let's be as thorough in our private efforts because a spirit of excellence flows between our private and public lives. If you're diligent at your job, why not emulate that at home? Do not shortchange your spouse and children while giving your boss or company chief executive officer your best. Be impactful wherever you go. Why?

Effective communication in private or business circles sets you apart from the pack, not that you are trying to be different or unique. Nevertheless, it distinguishes you as a person of quality. Anyone can talk, but not many communicate or know how.

Talking is an instinct and rote act, whereas communicating is calculated—you determine and practice to be a better communicator. For illustration, an 18-month-old toddler knows how to talk, but we may not understand them clearly for some time. There are sounds resembling words, but the sound isn't articulated. The potential is there but untapped. The same applies to us older folk. Even those who feel they have a good grasp and are communicating might not be doing it as efficiently as possible.

Effective communication in private or business circles sets you apart from the crowd.

There's always room for growth. This book is a start for those who have not thought about what they say or how it's received, for individuals who feel they're already skilled in this area, and for those who do it for a living. You can be a communications major, a public speaker, a pastor, or a teacher, but you still need improvement. What matters is that we never stop learning and growing. No one knows it all.

My mission is accomplished when you close this book with a renewed outlook and knowledge about *your* communication skills and begin thinking before you speak. When you hit pause or stop instead of play, you are ready to engage with and develop a creative and fruitful communication lifestyle.

If by some chance you haven't noticed it yet, the principles of T-H-I-N-K are interdependent. This means they work in tandem and are not independent of the other. When you speak truthfully, you are helpful. When you are helpful, you inspire. Inspiring dialog is essential to the receiver as it builds up versus destroying them. If the words are needed, that means they will be kind. Kind words are always on time and in season.

Parting Words

Remember to think. You're on the brink of a breakthrough. Having mastered the old, you're on to bigger and better and can't afford irresponsible or risky behavior. Occasions will arise, and temptations will be plentiful, but we will be ready, yes? Gone are the days of speaking impulsively and dealing with the consequences later.

That is the old you. The new you is aware and mindful. We are striving for a new mindset, a shift in the right direction. Does this mean you won't slip and fall? NO! If you revert to the old you, don't despair. Get up, dust yourself off, and try again—no self-condemnation. As with life, you'll make mistakes. Learn to forgive yourself, realize your error, grow from it, and improve. I keep repeating that, but it bears reiterating.

This is a new season, a new era. Let's be bold and courageous in the purpose of God for our life. We are winning from here on out. That winning formula is:

Be Truthful, Be Helpful, Be Inspiring, Ask yourself if it's Necessary, and Be Kind!

REFERENCES

Cambridge University Press & Assessment. (2024, October 6th). *Punch Down*. Retrieved from https://dictionary.cambridge.org/us/dictionary: https://dictionary.cambridge.org/dictionary/english/punch-down

Mental Health: Strengthening Our Response. (2022, June 17th). Retrieved from World Health Organization International: https://www.who.int/news-room/fact-sheets/detail/mental-health-strengthening-our-response

Merriam Webster. (2024, September 13th). Retrieved from Merriam-Webster.com: https://www.merriam-webster.com/dictionary/helpful

Merriam Webster. (2024, September 11th). *Merriam-Webster*. Retrieved from Merriam-Webster.com: https://www.merriam-webster.com/dictionary/inspire

Merriam Webster. (2024, September 4th). *merriam-webster.com/dictionary/true*. Retrieved from https://www.merriam-webster.com/: https://www.merriam-webster.com/dictionary/true

Merriam-Webster. (2024, September 14th). *Merriam-Webster*. Retrieved from Merriam-Webster.com: https://www.merriam-webster.com/dictionary/necessary

Merriam-Webster. (2024, September 9th). *Merriam-Webster.com*. Retrieved from Merriam-Webster.com: https://www.merriam-webster.com/dictionary/kind

Merriam-Webster.com. (2024, September 14th). Retrieved from Merriam-Webster.com: https://www.merriam-webster.com/dictionary/necessary

Merriam-Webster.com. (2024, September 16th). *merriam-webster.com/dictionary/indignation*. Retrieved from Merriam-Webster.com: https://www.merriam-webster.com/dictionary/indignation

Ni, P. (2015, Jul 12th). *Top 10 Reasons Relationships Fail*. Retrieved from PsychologyToday.com: https://www.psychologytoday.com/us/blog/communication-success/201507/top-10-reasons-relationships-fail

University of Rochester Medical Center. (2022, December 12th). *"Researchers reveal how trauma changes the brain."*. Retrieved from Science Daily: https://www.sciencedaily.com/releases/2022/12/221207142255.htm

WebMD Editorial Contributors. (2024, February 29th). *What to Know About Emotional Health*. Retrieved from webmd.com: https://www.webmd.com/balance/what-to-know-about-emotional-health

ABOUT THE AUTHOR

Pamela D. Foster is a proud retired Air Force military veteran. She holds a B.A. in Human Services and an M.A. in Human Relations from the University of Oklahoma. For over twenty years, she has been involved in Christian ministry leadership and youth mentoring and is a strong advocate for adolescent stewardship. In her spare time, she enjoys traveling overseas and reading thrillers and cozy mysteries.

For more information about Pamela, please visit:
Twitter – @PamelaDFos

Thank you so much for reading

I hope you enjoyed this short but insightful book as much as I enjoyed writing it. If you enjoyed it, please leave your comment and/or a book review at your favorite online book retailer(s).

Warm Regards,

Pamela D. Foster

****

You can subscribe to my Amazon Author Central page while you are at it.

Go to http://www.pameladfoster.com for additional information and events.

www.ingramcontent.com/pod-product-compliance
Lightning Source LLC
Chambersburg PA
CBHW070603010526
44118CB00012B/1433